AYRAA BERNARD

BUCHAREST TRAVEL GUIDE

Your Guide to Romania's Vibrant Capital including the History, Time zone, Must-see Attractions, Accomodations and Transportation

First edition

This book was professionally typeset on Reedsy.
Find out more at reedsy.com

This guide extends an invitation, a whispered assurance of enchantment awaiting at every turn. It speaks to dreamers, wanderers, romantics, and rebels, those who recognize a city as more than bricks and mortar but a living tapestry woven from laughter, tears, passion, and resilience.

So, peruse its pages, dear traveler, and let Bucharest confide its secrets in your ear. This guide is your key, your passport to a city that will allure you with its beauty.

Contents

1

Chapter 1

Introduction to Bucharest

- Overview of the City

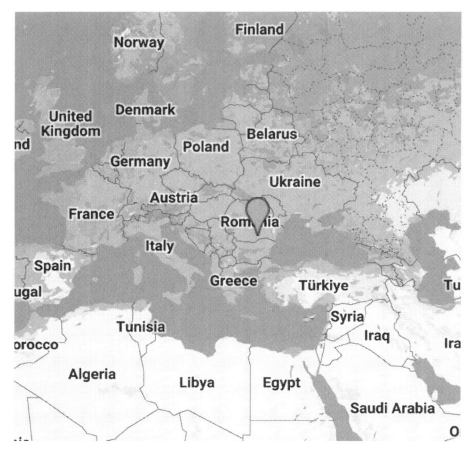

Map of Romania

Bucharest, the vibrant capital of Romania, is a city that pulsates with energy and intrigue. It's a place where grand boulevards lined with Belle Époque mansions meet gritty communist-era blocks, where ancient churches whisper of Byzantine eras and sleek skyscrapers pierce the sky. It's a city that's both glamorous and chaotic, sophisticated and raw, and it's this very juxtaposition that makes it so captivating.

Map of Bucharest, Romania

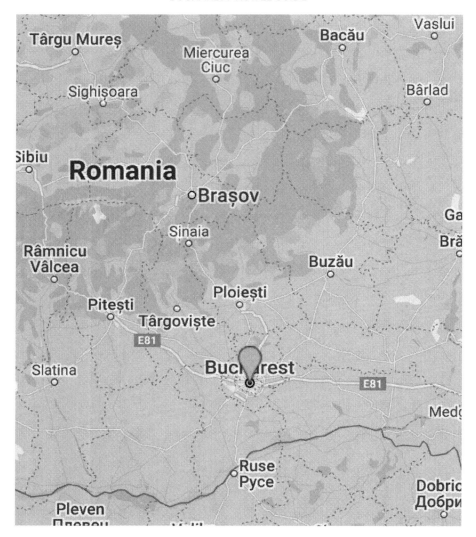

Map of Bucharest, Romania

A Historical Tapestry: Bucharest's history is a rich tapestry woven from threads of conquest, revolution, and artistic flourish. Founded in the 15th century, the city has been shaped by countless hands, from Ottoman sultans to Romanian revolutionaries, leaving behind a tangible legacy in its architectural styles.

Lipscani

- **Palace of Parliament:** The opulent behemoth that dominates the city center is a stark reminder of the Ceausescu era. While its grandeur is undeniable, its oppressive history casts a long shadow.

Palace of Parliament

- **Curtea Veche:** This 15th-century Princely Court, nestled amidst modern buildings, whispers tales of Bucharest's medieval beginnings.
- **Stavropoleos Church:** This intricately carved masterpiece of Byzantine architecture is a hidden gem tucked away in the Old Town, its beauty transporting you to another era.

Cultural Kaleidoscope: Bucharest's cultural scene is as diverse as its architecture. From world-class museums and grand opera houses to lively street art and underground music venues, the city caters to every taste.

- **National Museum of Art of Romania:** Housing an impressive collection of Romanian and European art, this museum is a must-see for art lovers.
- **Romanian Athenaeum:** This neoclassical concert hall, with its exquisite acoustics, is the heart of Bucharest's musical scene.

Romanian Athenaeum

- **Pasajul Victoria:** This 19th-century arcade, now home to quirky shops and cafes, is a charming escape from the bustle of the city.

Gastronomic Delights: Bucharest's culinary scene is a delicious blend of traditional Romanian fare and international influences. From hearty stews and grilled meats to fresh salads and modern fusion cuisine, there's something to tantalize every palate.

- **Sarmale:** These cabbage rolls stuffed with rice and meat are a national dish, best enjoyed with a dollop of sour cream.
- **Ciorbă:** This sour soup, often featuring vegetables or tripe, is a refreshing and flavorful starter.
- **Micii:** These small grilled sausages are a street food staple, perfect for a quick bite on the go.

Beyond the City Center: Venture beyond the city center and you'll discover hidden gems like:

- **Herastrau Park:** This sprawling green oasis, with its lake, gardens, and amusement park, is a welcome escape from the urban jungle.

Herăstrau Park

- **Village Museum:** This open-air museum showcases traditional Romanian houses and crafts, offering a glimpse into the country's rich heritage.
- **Snagov Monastery:** This 15th-century monastery, located on a picturesque island lake, is a haven of peace and tranquility.

Bucharest is a city that defies easy definition. It's a city that will surprise you, challenge you, and ultimately, leave you enchanted. So, pack your bags, embrace the contrasts, and get ready to discover the magic of Bucharest.

- Brief History

Bucharest, the captivating capital of Romania, boasts a history as rich and multifaceted as its architecture. From humble beginnings to opulent grandeur, the city has weathered centuries of conquests, revolutions, and artistic flourishes, leaving behind a captivating tapestry of eras and influences. Let's embark on a whirlwind journey through time, tracing the key chapters that shaped Bucharest into the vibrant metropolis it is today.

Early Traces: Archaeological whispers suggest settlements in the Bucharest area as far back as the Paleolithic period. Traces of Neolithic dwellings have been unearthed, hinting at the city's ancient roots.

Medieval Beginnings: The first documented mention of Bucharest dates back to 1459, appearing in a letter by the infamous Vlad III Dracula (yes, *that* Dracula!). It served as a summer residence for the Wallachian princes, eventually becoming a fortified citadel and a crucial trade hub.

Ottoman Influence: The 16th century saw the Ottomans rise to power, and Bucharest fell under their rule for several centuries. This era brought significant change, with mosques and Turkish baths dotting the cityscape, a legacy still visible today in landmarks like the Carol Mosque.

A City Flourishes: Following the decline of Ottoman power, Bucharest blossomed in the 18th and 19th centuries. Trade flourished, grand palaces were erected, and the city embraced Western European architectural styles, particularly Belle Époque, giving rise to stunning boulevards and ornate mansions.

Revolution and Change: The 20th century ushered in dramatic shifts. World War I and the subsequent rise of communism drastically altered the city's landscape. Ceausescu's megalomaniacal reign left its mark with the colossal Palace of Parliament, a controversial symbol of both grandeur and oppression.

Modern Bucharest: Today, Bucharest is a city in flux. While the scars of the past remain, a vibrant energy pulsates through its streets. Modern skyscrapers mingle with historical landmarks, bustling markets overflow with fresh produce, and trendy cafes spill onto cobbled alleyways.

This brief overview merely scratches the surface of Bucharest's rich history. From medieval intrigue to communist grandeur, the city's past whispers in every corner, waiting to be unraveled by curious explorers. So, delve deeper, wander its streets, and discover the captivating layers that make Bucharest a truly unique and unforgettable destination.

- Why Visit Bucharest

Bucharest, the vibrant capital of Romania, is often overlooked by travelers in favor of its flashier European counterparts. However, this hidden gem pulsates with energy, charm, and historical intrigue, offering a unique and affordable urban adventure. Here are 10 reasons why Bucharest should be your next travel destination:

1. Architectural Tapestry: Bucharest's skyline is a mesmerizing blend of architectural styles, from grand Belle Époque mansions like Cantacuzene Palace to the opulent neoclassical Romanian Athenaeum and the imposing Palace of Parliament, a behemoth of communist-era grandeur.

2. Historical Crossroads: Immerse yourself in Bucharest's rich history, from the medieval whispers of Curtea Veche, the former Princely Court, to the Byzantine majesty of Stavropoleos Church and the remnants of Ceausescu's regime.

3. Cultural Kaleidoscope: Explore world-class museums like the National Museum of Art of Romania, discover vibrant street art in hidden alleys, or lose yourself in the melodies of the Romanian Athenaeum.

4. Gastronomic Delights: Indulge in traditional Romanian fare like hearty stews, grilled meats, and the ubiquitous sarmale (cabbage rolls), or tantalize your taste buds with modern fusion cuisine and fresh local produce.

5. Lively Nightlife: From trendy rooftop bars and underground music venues to bustling pubs and intimate jazz clubs, Bucharest's nightlife caters to every taste, pulsing with energy until the early hours.

6. Green Oasis Escape: Take a break from the urban jungle in Herastrau Park, Bucharest's sprawling green haven with a lake, gardens, and amusement park, or explore the charming Village Museum, showcasing traditional Romanian houses and crafts.

7. Day Trips Delight: Venture beyond the city center and discover hidden gems like Snagov Monastery, a tranquil island retreat, or Bran Castle, perched high on a hill, forever linked to the legend of Dracula.

8. Affordability: Bucharest offers incredible value for money, with delicious meals, budget-friendly accommodation, and cheap public transportation, making it an ideal destination for backpackers and budget travelers.

9. Warm Hospitality: Romanians are known for their warmth and hospitality, always willing to help you navigate the city, recommend hidden gems, and share their love for their country.

10. Unforgettable Experience: Bucharest is a city that will surprise you, challenge you, and ultimately leave you enchanted. Its unique blend of history, culture, affordability, and charm guarantees an unforgettable travel experience.

So, pack your bags, embrace the contrasts, and get ready to discover the magic of Bucharest, a city that will steal your heart, one cobblestone street at a time.

Bonus Tip: Learn a few basic Romanian phrases - "Bună ziua" (Good day), "Mulțumesc" (Thank you), and "Vă rog" (Please) - to add a touch of charm to your interactions and impress the locals.

2

Chapter 2

Planning Your Trip

- Time zone in Bucharest

A s of right now, Friday, January 12, 2024, at 9:04 AM PST, Bucharest is currently in Eastern European Time (EET), which is 7 hours ahead of Coordinated Universal Time (UTC). This means that in Bucharest, it is currently 4:04 PM.

It's important to keep in mind that daylight saving time may affect the time zone in Bucharest at different times of the year. However, right now, it is in EET.

- Best Time to Visit

Bucharest is a vibrant city with something to offer visitors year-round, but the best time to visit really depends on what you're looking for in your trip. Here's a breakdown of the pros and cons of each season:

Spring (April-May):

- **Pros:** Pleasant weather with sunny skies and comfortable temperatures, perfect for exploring the city on foot or bike. Fewer crowds than summer, making it easier to find accommodation and navigate attractions. Beautiful blooming flowers in parks and gardens.
- **Cons:** Some rainy days are possible, although less likely than in autumn. May 1st is a national holiday, so many Romanians leave the city, making it somewhat quieter but also potentially impacting some opening hours.

Summer (June-August):

- **Pros:** Warmest weather of the year, ideal for enjoying outdoor activities like swimming, sunbathing, and picnicking in parks. Lively atmosphere with plenty of festivals and events happening throughout the city. Long days with plenty of daylight hours for sightseeing.
- **Cons:** Can get very hot and humid, especially in July and August. Tourist crowds at their peak, so expect higher prices and longer queues at popular attractions.

Autumn (September-November):

- **Pros:** Pleasant weather with warm days and cool nights, perfect for outdoor activities without the summer heat. Beautiful fall foliage in parks and gardens. Fewer crowds than in summer, making it easier to find deals on accommodation and activities. Rich cultural season with many concerts, exhibitions, and theater performances.

- **Cons:** More rainy days than spring or summer, although not enough to spoil your trip. Some attractions may have shorter opening hours.

Winter (December-March):

- **Pros:** Cheapest time to visit Bucharest, with great deals on flights and accommodation. Fewer crowds at tourist attractions. Magical Christmas atmosphere with festive decorations and markets. Cozy cafes and pubs perfect for escaping the cold weather.
- **Cons:** Coldest weather of the year, with potential for snow and ice. Some outdoor activities may not be available. Shorter days with less daylight for sightseeing.

Ultimately, the best time to visit Bucharest depends on your personal preferences and priorities. If you're looking for warm weather and outdoor activities, summer is the best choice. If you prefer cooler temperatures and fewer crowds, spring or autumn are ideal. And if you're on a budget and don't mind the cold, winter can be a great time to visit.

Here are some additional factors to consider when deciding when to visit Bucharest:

- **Events and festivals:** Bucharest hosts a variety of events and festivals throughout the year, so you may want to plan your trip around a specific event that interests you.
- **Prices:** Prices for flights and accommodation are generally highest in summer and lowest in winter.
- **Your personal preferences:** Do you prefer hot or cold weather? Do you mind crowds? Once you consider these factors, you can choose the best time to visit Bucharest for you.

- Duration of Stay

The ideal duration of your stay in Bucharest depends on your travel style and interests. Here's a breakdown to help you decide:

Short Stay (1-2 days):

- Perfect for a quick city break or weekend getaway.
- Focus on the highlights like the Palace of Parliament, Old Town, and Herastrau Park.
- Experience the city's vibrant nightlife and pub scene.
- Enjoy delicious Romanian cuisine at traditional restaurants.

Moderate Stay (3-5 days):

- Allows you to delve deeper into Bucharest's history and culture.
- Visit museums like the National Museum of Art of Romania and the Village Museum.
- Take a day trip to Bran Castle (Dracula's Castle) or Snagov Monastery.
- Explore hidden gems like Pasajul Victoria and Curtea Veche.

Extended Stay (1 week or more):

- Immerse yourself in the local life and rhythm of the city.
- Discover off-the-beaten-path neighborhoods and cafes.
- Learn a few basic Romanian phrases to connect with locals.
- Take cooking classes and learn to prepare traditional dishes.
- Attend local festivals and cultural events.

Bonus Tip: Consider purchasing the Bucharest City Card for free public transportation, discounts on attractions, and skip-the-line access to some museums.

Ultimately, the best way to decide how long to stay in Bucharest is to listen to your own travel desires. If you're looking for a whirlwind city break, 1-2 days may be enough. But if you want to truly experience the magic of Bucharest, consider staying for at least 3-5 days or even longer.

- Travel Essentials

Bucharest, the captivating capital of Romania, awaits with open arms and hidden gems for you to discover. But before you embark on your adventure, packing the right travel essentials is key to maximizing your experience. Here's a handy list to guide you:

Essentials for All Seasons:

- **Comfortable walking shoes:** Bucharest is best explored on foot, so pack sturdy shoes that can handle cobblestone streets and long walks.
- **Weather-appropriate clothing:** Bucharest's weather can be unpredictable, so consider layering options for all seasons. Pack a light jacket for spring and autumn, a raincoat for occasional showers, and a warm coat and hat for winter. In summer, pack breathable clothing for the heat.
- **Universal adapter:** Romania uses Type F power plugs, so pack a universal adapter to keep your devices charged.
- **Romanian phrasebook (optional):** While many Romanians speak English, learning a few basic phrases like "Bună ziua" (Good day), "Mulțumesc" (Thank you), and "Vă rog" (Please) can go a long way.
- **Reusable water bottle:** Staying hydrated is important, so pack a reusable water bottle to fill up instead of buying plastic bottles.

- **Sunscreen and sunglasses (summer):** Summer in Bucharest can be sunny, so protect your skin and eyes with sunscreen and sunglasses.

Additional Essentials for Specific Activities:

- **Swimsuit and towel:** If you plan on visiting swimming pools or enjoying Herastrau Park's lake, pack a swimsuit and towel.
- **Hiking boots (optional):** If you're planning on doing any hiking or exploring nature outside the city, pack a good pair of hiking boots.
- **Camera:** Capture Bucharest's beauty and charm with a camera or your phone.
- **Books and entertainment:** For leisurely evenings or long journeys, pack a book or download some movies or music to keep you entertained.

Documents and Important Items:

- **Passport and visa (if required):** Ensure your passport is valid for travel and check visa requirements for Romania.
- **Travel insurance:** Get travel insurance to protect yourself against unexpected events like flight cancellations or medical emergencies.
- **Photocopies of important documents:** Make copies of your passport, visa, and travel insurance for safekeeping.
- **Credit cards and cash:** Bucharest accepts credit cards at most places, but it's always good to have some cash on hand for emergencies or smaller purchases.
- **Medications:** If you take any prescription medications, pack enough for your trip and bring a doctor's note if necessary.

Bonus Tips:

- Download offline maps or Google Translate to help you navigate the city.
- Pack light clothing that can be easily mixed and matched to create different outfits.

- Leave some space in your luggage for souvenirs!

By packing these essentials, you'll be well-equipped to explore Bucharest and create unforgettable memories in this vibrant city. Remember, the most important thing is to pack your sense of adventure and an open mind. Have a wonderful trip!

Additional Tips:

- Consider purchasing the Bucharest City Card for free public transportation, discounts on attractions, and skip-the-line access to some museums.
- Learn a few basic Romanian phrases to connect with locals.
- Don't be afraid to venture beyond the city center and explore hidden gems. Bucharest has something for everyone!

3

Chapter 3

Getting to Bucharest

- Transportation Options

Bucharest, the captivating capital of Romania, welcomes travelers with open arms and a fascinating tapestry of experiences. But before you embark on your adventure, choosing the right way to get there is crucial. Here's a breakdown of various transportation options to suit your budget, timeframe, and travel style:

Flying High:

- **The fastest and most convenient option:** Bucharest Henri Coandă International Airport (OTP) is the main gateway to the city, with connections to numerous European and international destinations.
- **Flight time:** Varies depending on your origin, but expect journeys between 2-5 hours from major European cities.
- **Cost:** Can be expensive, especially during peak season. Compare prices across different airlines and booking platforms to find the best deals.
- **Airport transfer:** Public transport options like buses and the Metro are

available, but taxis and ride-sharing services offer more comfort and convenience.

Taking the Train:

- **A scenic and budget-friendly alternative:** Train journeys from neighboring European countries like Hungary, Austria, and Serbia offer a glimpse into the region's landscapes and charm.
- **Travel time:** Can be significantly longer than flying, ranging from 8-24 hours depending on the route.
- **Cost:** Generally cheaper than airfare, especially if you book in advance or travel during off-peak seasons.
- **Comfort:** Train travel can be quite comfortable, with modern sleeper trains and scenic routes available.

Rolling In by Bus:

- **The most budget-conscious option:** Bus journeys from nearby European cities like Vienna, Budapest, and Belgrade offer an affordable way to reach Bucharest.
- **Travel time:** Similar to train travel, ranging from 8-24 hours depending on the route and number of stops.
- **Cost:** Often the cheapest option, especially for budget travelers and backpackers.
- **Comfort:** Bus travel can vary depending on the company and route. Choose reputable operators with modern coaches for a comfortable journey.

Hitting the Road:

- **For the adventurous souls:** Driving to Bucharest from neighboring countries can be a rewarding experience, allowing you to stop at scenic villages and attractions along the way.

- **Travel time:** Varies depending on your origin and planned route. Expect at least 8-12 hours from major European cities.
- **Cost:** Depends on fuel costs, car rentals (if applicable), and potential border crossing fees.
- **Preparation:** Ensure your car has the necessary paperwork and roadworthiness certificates for crossing borders.

Once You Arrive:

- **Public transportation:** Bucharest boasts a comprehensive network of buses, trams, and the Metro, offering affordable and convenient ways to get around the city.
- **Taxis and ride-sharing:** Taxis and ride-sharing apps like Uber and Bolt are readily available and offer a comfortable way to get to your destination, especially with luggage.
- **Walking and cycling:** Exploring Bucharest on foot or by bike is a great way to experience the city's atmosphere and hidden gems. Many areas are pedestrian-friendly and bike rentals are available.

Bonus Tip: Consider purchasing the Bucharest City Card for free public transportation, discounts on attractions, and skip-the-line access to some museums.

- Arriving by Air

Arriving By Air at Bucharest:

Reaching Henri Coandă International Airport (OTP):

- **Airlines:** Bucharest Henri Coandă International Airport is well-connected, with major airlines like Lufthansa, Turkish Airlines, Ryanair, TAROM, and Wizz Air offering flights from numerous European and international destinations.
- **Flight Information:** Check websites like Skyscanner, Google Flights, or directly with airlines for the best deals and flight options based on your origin and travel dates.
- **Visa Requirements:** Check visa requirements for Romania based on your nationality well in advance. Some nationalities may require visas for entry.
- **Passport and Travel Documents:** Ensure your passport is valid and you have all necessary travel documents, including boarding passes, visa (if required), and travel insurance.

Navigating the Airport:

- **Arrival Terminals:** Bucharest Henri Coandă Airport has two arrival terminals: Terminal 1 for international flights and Terminal 2 for domestic and regional flights.
- **Immigration and Customs:** Prepare to go through immigration and customs upon arrival. Follow airport signs and instructions from officials.
- **Currency Exchange:** Several currency exchange booths are available in the arrivals area. Consider exchanging some money for immediate needs like taxis or public transportation.
- **Baggage Claim:** Collect your luggage at the designated baggage claim area for your arrival terminal.
- **Connecting Flights:** If you have a connecting flight within Romania,

follow signs or ask airport staff for assistance to reach the transfer area.

Transportation Options from the Airport:

- **Public Transportation:** Bucharest offers a convenient and affordable public transport system. Take the Express RATB Bus 783 directly to the city center (Piata Unirii). Other bus and Metro options are available as well.
- **Taxis and Ride-sharing:** Taxis and ride-sharing apps like Uber and Bolt are readily available at the airport. Taxis offer a convenient option, while ride-sharing can be cheaper if booked in advance.
- **Rental Cars:** Car rental companies operate at the airport if you prefer exploring Romania on your own wheels. Make sure you have the necessary paperwork and meet rental requirements.

- Arriving by Car

Arriving in Bucharest by car can be a fantastic way to soak in the sights and flexibility of exploring at your own pace. Here's what you need to know for a smooth road trip to the charming Romanian capital:

Planning Your Route:

- **Origin:** Knowing your starting point helps determine the best route considering road conditions, border crossings, and estimated travel time.
- **Navigation:** Invest in a reliable GPS or download offline maps of Romania and neighboring countries you'll traverse.

- **Permits and Documents:** Ensure you have all necessary documents like your passport, driving license, car registration, and international driving permit (if required).
- **Vignettes:** Purchase motorway vignettes for countries with toll roads like Hungary and Austria before entering.

Hitting the Road:

- **Road Conditions:** Research road conditions on your chosen route. Some stretches might require extra caution or detours.
- **Border Crossings:** Be prepared for possible queues and checks at border crossings. Have your documents readily available.
- **Rest Stops and Fuel:** Factor in breaks and gas station stops, especially on long journeys. Research rest areas along your route.
- **Traffic Laws:** Familiarize yourself with Romanian traffic regulations. Speed limits, alcohol restrictions, and other rules differ from your home country.

Arriving in Bucharest:

- **Parking:** Research parking options depending on your accommodation and planned activities. Consider underground parking garages or designated parking zones.
- **City Navigation:** Familiarize yourself with Bucharest's traffic grid and one-way streets. Maps and navigation apps can be helpful.
- **Public Transportation:** If venturing deeper into the city, Bucharest boasts a reliable public transport network with buses, trams, and the Metro.
- **Day Trips:** Your car gives you access to exciting day trips around Bucharest. Explore charming towns like Sibiu, Brasov, or Bran Castle at your own pace.

Bonus Tips:

- Learn some basic Romanian phrases for greetings and essentials. Locals appreciate the effort!
- Pack snacks and drinks for the journey, especially if traveling with children.
- Consider international roaming packages for your phone if needed.
- Download audiobooks or podcasts for entertainment during long stretches.
- Most importantly, relax, enjoy the scenery, and embrace the adventure of a road trip to Bucharest!

Have a wonderful road trip and a memorable stay in Bucharest!

- Public Transportation

Ah, the budget-friendly and often scenic route! Arriving in Bucharest by public transportation can be a rewarding experience, immersing you in the local rhythm and offering affordable access to the city. Here's a guide to smooth arrivals via bus, train, or even ship, depending on your origin and preferences:

By Bus:

- **Extensive Network:** Bucharest is well-connected by bus routes from numerous European cities like Vienna, Budapest, Belgrade, and Sofia.
- **Cost-Effective:** Bus travel is often the cheapest option, especially for budget travelers and backpackers.
- **Travel Time:** Expect journeys between 8-24 hours depending on the route and number of stops.

- **Comfort:** Bus comfort varies depending on the company and route. Choose reputable operators with modern coaches for a smoother ride.
- **Helpful Tips:** Book tickets in advance for popular routes and during peak season. Pack snacks and drinks for long journeys. Download offline maps or Google Translate for assistance.

By Train:

- **Scenic Journeys:** Train travel offers the chance to admire picturesque landscapes and charming towns along the way.
- **Diverse Options:** Train connections are available from neighboring countries like Hungary, Austria, Serbia, and even some further destinations.
- **Travel Time:** Similar to bus travel, expect journeys between 8-24 hours depending on the route and connections.
- **Comfort:** Train travel can be quite comfortable, with modern sleeper trains and scenic routes available.
- **Helpful Tips:** Purchase tickets early for the best deals and secure your preferred cabin or seat. Pack essentials for overnight journeys. Consider international roaming packages for your phone if needed.

By Ship (for the Adventurous):

- **Unique Experience:** If arriving from countries bordering the Black Sea like Bulgaria or Ukraine, consider the adventurous option of a ferry to Constanța, followed by a short train or bus journey to Bucharest.
- **Travel Time:** Varies depending on your origin and ferry schedule. Be prepared for longer travel times compared to land options.
- **Uniqueness:** Enjoy the sea breeze and scenic sights during the ferry journey. This option offers a truly unique entry point to Romania.
- **Helpful Tips:** Check ferry schedules and book tickets in advance, especially during peak season. Research immigration procedures and visa requirements for entering Romania via Constanța.

Once You Arrive:

- **Public Transportation:** Bucharest boasts a comprehensive network of buses, trams, and the Metro, offering affordable and convenient ways to get around the city. Purchase a travel card for multiple journeys at discounted rates.
- **Taxis and Ride-sharing:** Taxis and ride-sharing apps like Uber and Bolt are readily available at bus and train stations. Consider this option for convenience, especially with luggage.
- **Walking and Cycling:** Exploring Bucharest on foot or by bike is a great way to experience the city's atmosphere and hidden gems. Many areas are pedestrian-friendly and bike rentals are available.

4

Chapter 4

Accommodation

- Types of Accommodation

Bucharest, the vibrant capital of Romania, offers a diverse range of accommodation options to suit all budgets and travel styles. Whether you're a solo backpacker, a couple on a romantic getaway, a family with kids, or a group of friends exploring the city, you'll find a perfect place to rest your head and recharge for your Romanian adventures.

Here's a breakdown of some popular types of accommodation in Bucharest:

For the Budget-Conscious:

- **Hostels:** Bucharest boasts a lively hostel scene, with affordable bunk beds in dormitory-style rooms or private rooms for solo travelers or couples. Hostels often offer common areas for socializing, shared kitchens, and even organized activities, making them a great option for meeting fellow travelers.
- **Guesthouses:** Family-run guesthouses offer cozy and budget-friendly

stays with a personal touch. Expect comfortable rooms, sometimes with shared bathrooms, and a more local experience compared to larger hotels.

- **Apartments:** Renting an apartment through platforms like Airbnb can be a cost-effective option for groups or families. You'll enjoy the privacy and space of your own place, complete with a kitchen and living area.

For the Comfort Seekers:

- **Hotels:** Bucharest has a wide range of hotels to choose from, from affordable chains to luxurious five-star establishments. Consider your budget, location preference, and desired amenities like spas, gyms, or rooftop pools when making your choice.
- **Boutique Hotels:** For a more intimate and personalized experience, opt for a boutique hotel. These smaller establishments often have unique decor, charming courtyards, and attentive service.
- **Aparthotels:** Aparthotels combine the comfort of a hotel with the convenience of an apartment. Enjoy spacious rooms with kitchenettes or full kitchens, perfect for longer stays or families who prefer to prepare some meals themselves.

For the Unique Experience:

- **Historic Mansions:** Immerse yourself in Bucharest's history by staying in a restored historic mansion. These grand buildings offer luxurious accommodations and a glimpse into the city's past.
- **Castles and Cottages:** Venture beyond the city center and experience the rustic charm of staying in a Romanian castle or cottage. These unique accommodations offer picturesque surroundings and escape the urban buzz.
- **Glamping:** For nature lovers, glamping tents in the outskirts of Bucharest offer a comfortable and unique way to experience the Romanian countryside.

Remember, choosing the right accommodation depends on your priorities, budget, and desired level of comfort and independence. Don't hesitate to research different options and read reviews before making your booking. Bucharest has something for everyone, so find the perfect place to call home during your Romanian adventure!

- Top 10 Hotels in Bucharest

Here's a curated list of the top 10 hotels in Bucharest, catering to diverse budgets and travel styles:

1. JW Marriott Bucharest Grand Hotel:

- **Address:** Calea 13 Septembrie 90, Bucharest 010010, Romania
- **Phone:** +40 21 403 0000
- **Operation Hours:** 24/7
- **Price Range:** $$$$ (Luxury)
- **Highlights:** Elegant rooms and suites, 5 restaurants, a casino, spa with sauna, indoor and outdoor pools, stunning city views.

2. Radisson Blu Hotel, Bucharest:

- **Address:** Calea Victoriei 63-81, Bucharest 010001, Romania
- **Phone:** +40 21 311 9000
- **Operation Hours:** 24/7
- **Price Range:** $$$ (Luxury)
- **Highlights:** Sophisticated property with free Wi-Fi, indoor and outdoor

pools, spa, 5 restaurants, 3 bars, excellent location near landmarks.

3. Grand Hotel Bucharest:

- **Address:** Bulevardul Nicolae Bălcescu 4, Bucharest 010005, Romania
- **Phone:** +40 21 310 2020
- **Operation Hours:** 24/7
- **Price Range:** $$$ (Luxury)
- **Highlights:** Posh rooms and suites, refined dining, 22nd-floor indoor pool, panoramic city views, conference facilities, spa.

4. Athénée Palace Hotel Bucharest:

- **Address:** Strada Episcopul Radu 1, Bucharest 010006, Romania
- **Phone:** +40 21 314 0000
- **Operation Hours:** 24/7
- **Price Range:** $$$ (Luxury)
- **Highlights:** Neoclassical architecture, elegant interiors, renowned Caru' Cu Bere restaurant, live music bar, spa, fitness center, central location near the Athenaeum.

5. InterContinental Bucharest City Centre:

- **Address:** Strada Nicolae Bălcescu 19-21, Bucharest 010005, Romania
- **Phone:** +40 21 302 0000
- **Operation Hours:** 24/7
- **Price Range:** $$$ (Luxury)
- **Highlights:** Modern design, spacious rooms, rooftop bar with city views, spa, fitness center, excellent location near Victoriei Square.

6. The Mansion Bucharest:

- **Address:** Strada Popa Socolescu 3-5, Bucharest 010004, Romania

- **Phone:** +40 21 330 5533
- **Operation Hours:** 24/7
- **Price Range:** $$ (Mid-range)
- **Highlights:** Charming boutique hotel in a restored historic mansion, intimate atmosphere, personalized service, rooftop terrace, gourmet restaurant, central location near Old Town.

7. Hotel Carol Parc Bucharest:

- **Address:** Bulevardul Carol I 1-3, Bucharest 030167, Romania
- **Phone:** +40 21 319 0100
- **Operation Hours:** 24/7
- **Price Range:** $$ (Mid-range)
- **Highlights:** Family-friendly hotel with spacious rooms and apartments, indoor and outdoor pools, playground, kids' club, spa, fitness center, beautiful location in Carol Park.

8. Rembrandt Bucharest:

- **Address:** Strada Șelari 14, Bucharest 010003, Romania
- **Phone:** +40 21 314 0888
- **Operation Hours:** 24/7
- **Price Range:** $$ (Mid-range)
- **Highlights:** Stylish boutique hotel

9. Novotel Bucharest City Centre:

- **Address:** Calea Victoriei 107, Bucharest 010001, Romania
- **Phone:** +40 21 408 7800
- **Operation Hours:** 24/7
- **Price Range:** $ (Budget-friendly)
- **Highlights:** Modern and affordable hotel, central location near landmark attractions, spacious rooms with comfortable beds, family-friendly

facilities, restaurant, bar, meeting rooms.

10. ibis Styles Bucharest City Center:

- **Address:** Strada Șelari 5-7, Bucharest 010003, Romania
- **Phone:** +40 21 301 1286
- **Operation Hours:** 24/7
- **Price Range:** $ (Budget-friendly)
- **Highlights:** Vibrant and contemporary hotel, perfect for solo travelers and young couples, stylish rooms with quirky touches, central location near Old Town, café, bar, co-working space.

- Top Hostels in Bucharest

Here's a rundown of the top 10 hostels in Bucharest, catering to diverse preferences and travel styles:

1. The Old Thing Hostel:

- **Address:** Strada Popa Tătaru 3, Bucharest 010002, Romania
- **Phone:** +40 737 140 140
- **Price Range:** $ (Budget-friendly)
- **Highlights:** Centrally located in the historic Old Town, charming court-yard terrace, cozy common area with fireplace, movie nights and events, friendly staff, clean and comfortable beds.

2. Friends Hostel:

- **Address:** Strada Mircea Vulcănescu 114, Bucharest 010111, Romania
- **Price Range:** $ (Budget-friendly)
- **Highlights:** Laid-back atmosphere with friendly staff, spacious common area with games and activities, rooftop terrace with city views, comfortable dorms and private rooms, well-equipped kitchen, bar with happy hours, close to public transportation.

3. White Wall Hostel:

- **Address:** Strada Șelari 5, Bucharest 010003, Romania
- **Price Range:** $ (Budget-friendly)
- **Highlights:** Funky and colorful design, clean and comfortable dorms with privacy curtains, friendly staff, rooftop terrace with city views, free breakfast, well-equipped kitchen, central location near Old Town and nightlife.

4. Podstel Umbrella:

- **Address:** Strada Pisoni 26, Bucharest 030167, Romania
- **Price Range:** $$ (Mid-range)
- **Highlights:** Unique "pod" sleeping capsules offering privacy and comfort, trendy design, spacious common area with games and events, rooftop terrace with bar and city views, self-service laundry, close to Carol Park and public transportation.

5. Little Bucharest Old Town Hostel:

- **Address:** Strada Lipscani 79, Bucharest 030002, Romania
- **Price Range:** $$ (Mid-range)
- **Highlights:** Boutique-style hostel in a restored historic building, charming courtyard, comfortable dorms and private rooms with modern amenities, rooftop terrace with city views, friendly staff, excellent location in the heart of Old Town.

6. The Zip Hostel:

- **Address:** Strada Popa Socolescu 14, Bucharest 010004, Romania
- **Price Range:** $ (Budget-friendly)
- **Highlights:** Lively and social atmosphere, perfect for solo travelers, spacious common area with games and events, rooftop terrace with bar and city views, well-equipped kitchen, clean and comfortable dorms, central location near Old Town.

7. The Social Hostel Bucharest:

- **Address:** Strada Covaci 14, Bucharest 030002, Romania
- **Price Range:** $ (Budget-friendly)
- **Highlights:** Laid-back and welcoming atmosphere, friendly staff, comfortable dorms and private rooms with air conditioning, rooftop terrace with bar and city views, well-equipped kitchen, free breakfast, close to Old Town and nightlife.

8. Abraham Hostel Bucharest:

- **Address:** Strada Mihai Eminescu 89, Bucharest 010007, Romania
- **Price Range:** $$ (Mid-range)
- **Highlights:** Stylish and modern design, comfortable dorms and private rooms with en-suite bathrooms, rooftop terrace with bar and city views, well-equipped kitchen, free breakfast, laundry facilities, close to public transportation.

9. My Bucharest Hostel:

- **Address:** Strada Șelari 10, Bucharest 010003, Romania
- **Price Range:** $ (Budget-friendly)
- **Highlights:** Centrally located in Old Town, friendly and helpful staff, comfortable dorms and private rooms, rooftop terrace with city views,

well-equipped kitchen, laundry facilities, close to nightlife and attractions.

10. The House Hostel Bucharest:

- **Address:** Strada Popa Socolescu 12, Bucharest 010004, Romania
- **Phone:** +40 21 314 0825
- **Price Range:** $ (Budget-friendly)
- **Highlights:** Cozy and welcoming atmosphere, perfect for solo travelers and couples, comfortable dorms and private rooms with modern amenities, well-equipped kitchen, rooftop terrace with bar and city views, laundry facilities, close to Old Town and public transportation.

- Top 10 Guesthouses in Bucharest

Here's a glimpse into some of the top guesthouses in Bucharest, catering to diverse preferences and budgets:

1. Old Centrum Bucharest:

- **Address:** Strada Ioan Slavici 9A, Bucharest 010107, Romania
- **Phone:** +40 729 528 757
- **Price Range:** $$ (Mid-range)
- **Highlights:** Beautifully restored historic building in the heart of the Old Town, charming courtyard with seating, elegant and comfortable rooms with modern amenities, delicious breakfast included, friendly and helpful staff.

2. Central Guesthouse Bucharest:

- **Address:** Strada Bălcești 7, Bucharest 010005, Romania
- **Phone:** +40 757 056 620
- **Price Range:** $$ (Mid-range)
- **Highlights:** Convenient location near Victoriei Square and public transportation, spacious and clean rooms with shared or private bathrooms, cozy common area with fireplace, well-equipped kitchen, friendly staff offering local recommendations.

3. Casa Veche Carol Guesthouse:

- **Address:** Strada Carol Davila 38, Bucharest 010003, Romania
- **Phone:** +40 749 015 582
- **Price Range:** $ (Budget-friendly)
- **Highlights:** Peaceful location near Carol Park, family-run guesthouse with a warm atmosphere, comfortable and clean rooms, lovely garden with seating, shared kitchen, delicious homemade breakfast available.

4. Vila 18 Hotel Boutique:

- **Address:** Strada Dr. Iuliu Barasch 18, Bucharest 011924, Romania
- **Phone:** +40 727 296 084
- **Price Range:** $$ (Mid-range)
- **Highlights:** Elegant and stylish boutique guesthouse in a quiet residential area, spacious and modern rooms with balconies, friendly and attentive staff, delicious breakfast buffet, secure parking available.

5. Pensiunea La Noblesse:

- **Address:** Strada Barbu Știrbey 82, Bucharest 010006, Romania
- **Phone:** +40 788 680 577
- **Price Range:** $$ (Mid-range)

- **Highlights:** Charming building with Art Nouveau elements, panoramic rooftop terrace with city views, comfortable and well-equipped rooms, quiet and safe location near Kiseleff Park, helpful staff offering airport transfers.

6. Vila Zorba:

- **Address:** Strada Doctor Nicolae Kretzulescu 31, Bucharest 010003, Romania
- **Phone:** +40 728 105 889
- **Price Range:** $$ (Mid-range)
- **Highlights:** Traditional Romanian-style guesthouse with a garden, spacious and comfortable rooms with balconies, shared kitchen available, friendly and informative staff, close to public transportation and attractions.

7. Cazare Fundeni Medlife:

- **Address:** Strada Maior Eremia Grigorescu 33, Bucharest 030002, Romania
- **Phone:** +40 788 811 908
- **Price Range:** $ (Budget-friendly)
- **Highlights:** Modern and clean guesthouse near Carol Park, ideal for budget travelers, comfortable rooms with shared bathrooms, well-equipped kitchen, laundry facilities, friendly staff, good value for money.

8. Pensiunea Casa Verde Bucuresti:

- **Address:** Strada George Enescu 3, Bucharest 010001, Romania
- **Phone:** +40 723 479 776
- **Price Range:** $$ (Mid-range)
- **Highlights:** Quiet and green location near Victoriei Square, family-run guesthouse with a welcoming atmosphere, comfortable rooms with private bathrooms

9. Bucureşti Residence:

- **Address:** Strada Doctor N. Kretzulescu 58, Bucharest 010003, Romania
- **Phone:** +40 774 295 902
- **Price Range:** $$ (Mid-range)
- **Highlights:** Modern and elegant guesthouse in a quiet residential area, close to Herastrau Park, spacious and comfortable rooms with balconies, well-equipped kitchen available, secure parking, friendly staff offering local recommendations.

10. Guest House Victoria:

- **Address:** Strada General Berthelot 31, Bucharest 010006, Romania
- **Phone:** +40 751 542 641
- **Price Range:** $ (Budget-friendly)
- **Highlights:** Affordable guesthouse in a central location near Victoriei Square, perfect for solo travelers and backpackers, clean and basic rooms with shared bathrooms, shared kitchen available, friendly staff offering local tips, walking distance to major attractions.

- Top 10 Apartments in Bucharest

Here's a curated list of 10 top apartments in Bucharest, catering to diverse needs and preferences:

1. Old Town Gem:

- **Address:** Strada Lipscani 36, Bucharest 030002, Romania
- **Phone:** +40 733 056 928
- **Price Range:** $$$ (Luxury)
- **Highlights:** Historical building in the heart of Old Town, stylishly renovated interior, spacious 2-bedroom apartment with balcony and city views, fully equipped kitchen, modern bathroom, Wi-Fi, air conditioning, walkable to all major attractions.

2. Luxury Residence Piata Romana:

- **Address:** Piata Romana 3, Bucharest 010005, Romania
- **Phone:** +40 735 552 252
- **Price Range:** $$$ (Luxury)
- **Highlights:** Modern apartment building in a prestigious area, panoramic views of the city, 3-bedroom apartment with balcony and terrace, high-end furnishings, fully equipped kitchen, 2 bathrooms, Wi-Fi, air conditioning, concierge service, secure parking.

3. Cozy Nest near Carol Park:

- **Address:** Strada Carol Davila 30, Bucharest 010003, Romania
- **Phone:** +40 744 618 242
- **Price Range:** $$ (Mid-range)
- **Highlights:** Quiet location near Carol Park, bright and airy 1-bedroom apartment with balcony, modern furniture, fully equipped kitchen, washer/dryer, Wi-Fi, air conditioning, close to public transportation and green spaces.

4. Central Chic Studio:

- **Address:** Strada Calea Victoriei 116, Bucharest 010001, Romania

- **Phone:** +40 728 005 082
- **Price Range:** $$ (Mid-range)
- **Highlights:** Central location near Victoriei Square, stylish studio apartment with large window, comfortable bed, kitchenette, private bathroom, Wi-Fi, air conditioning, perfect for solo travelers or couples, walking distance to attractions.

5. Family-Friendly Apartment near Kiseleff Park:

- **Address:** Strada Dr. Iuliu Barasch 25, Bucharest 011924, Romania
- **Phone:** +40 733 532 956
- **Price Range:** $$ (Mid-range)
- **Highlights:** Quiet residential area near Kiseleff Park, spacious 3-bedroom apartment with balcony, fully equipped kitchen, 2 bathrooms, washing machine, Wi-Fi, air conditioning, ideal for families, close to parks and playgrounds.

6. Modern Oasis in Herastrau District:

- **Address:** Strada Dimitrie Suțu 15, Bucharest 011802, Romania
- **Phone:** +40 727 410 023
- **Price Range:** $$ (Mid-range)
- **Highlights:** Stylishly furnished 2-bedroom apartment in the prestigious Herastrau district, close to the lake and park, balcony with city views, fully equipped kitchen, 2 bathrooms, Wi-Fi, air conditioning, secure building with gym and pool access.

7. Budget-Friendly Studio in Old Town:

- **Address:** Strada Șelari 8, Bucharest 010003, Romania
- **Phone:** +40 730 097 052
- **Price Range:** $ (Budget-friendly)
- **Highlights:** Central location in Old Town, compact studio apartment with

41

kitchenette and private bathroom, Wi-Fi, air conditioning, perfect for budget-conscious solo travelers, close to nightlife and attractions.

8. Sunny Apartment with Terrace near Victoriei Square:

- **Address:** Strada General Berthelot 27, Bucharest 010006, Romania
- **Phone:** +40 730 550 529
- **Price Range:** $$ (Mid-range)
- **Highlights:** Central location near Victoriei Square, bright and spacious 2-bedroom apartment with private terrace, fully equipped kitchen, 2 bathrooms, Wi-Fi, air conditioning, close to public transportation and shops.

9. Bohemian Loft in Creative District:

- **Address:** Strada Mântuleasa 15, Bucharest 010006, Romania
- **Phone:** +40 722 529 405
- **Price Range:** $$ (Mid-range)
- **Highlights:** Unique apartment in a restored historical building in the trendy Mântuleasa district, industrial-chic interior with high ceilings, spacious mezzanine bedroom, fully equipped kitchen, open bathroom, Wi-Fi, air conditioning, perfect for creative couples or solo travelers, surrounded by galleries and cafes.

10. Green Retreat near Botanical Garden:

- **Address:** Strada Dr. Nicolae Kretzulescu 33, Bucharest 010003, Romania
- **Phone:** +40 736 128 540
- **Price Range:** $$ (Mid-range)
- **Highlights:** Peaceful location near the Botanical Garden, charming 1-bedroom apartment with balcony and garden view, well-equipped kitchen, spacious bathroom, Wi-Fi, air conditioning, walking distance to the garden and green spaces, ideal for nature lovers and those seeking a

quiet escape.

- Top 10 Aparthotels in Bucharest

Here's a curated list of 10 exceptional Bucharest aparthotels, catering to diverse needs and budgets:

1. Adagio Aparthotel Bucharest City Center:

- **Address:** Calea Victoriei 103-105, Bucharest 010001, Romania
- **Phone:** +40 21 302 0900
- **Price Range:** $$$ (Luxury)
- **Highlights:** Prime location in the heart of Bucharest, spacious and modern studios and apartments with fully equipped kitchens, daily housekeeping, on-site gym and spa, business center, panoramic rooftop terrace with city views.

2. The Charles Aparthotel:

- **Address:** Strada George Enescu 37, Bucharest 010001, Romania
- **Phone:** +40 21 303 5000
- **Price Range:** $$$ (Luxury)
- **Highlights:** Elegant aparthotel in a historic building near Victoriei Square, stylishly furnished apartments with fully equipped kitchens and balconies, 24-hour concierge service, gourmet on-site restaurant, fitness center, wellness area, rooftop terrace with city views.

3. Voila Aparthotel Floreasca:

- **Address:** Bulevardul Dimitrie Cantemir 11, Bucharest 030167, Romania
- **Phone:** +40 21 303 7500
- **Price Range:** $$ (Mid-range)
- **Highlights:** Modern and family-friendly aparthotel near Herastrau Park, spacious apartments with fully equipped kitchens and balconies, rooftop pool with city views, children's playground, on-site restaurant and cafe, parking available, close to green spaces and attractions.

4. Capital Plaza Aparthotel:

- **Address:** Strada Popa Socolescu 15, Bucharest 010004, Romania
- **Phone:** +40 21 314 0636
- **Price Range:** $$ (Mid-range)
- **Highlights:** Central location near the Old Town, comfortable and stylish studios and apartments with kitchenettes, on-site laundry facilities, rooftop terrace with city views, close to shops, restaurants, and attractions.

5. Bliss Aparthotel Bucharest:

- **Address:** Strada Mircea Vulcănescu 116, Bucharest 010111, Romania
- **Phone:** +40 21 317 6767
- **Price Range:** $$ (Mid-range)
- **Highlights:** Modern and contemporary aparthotel with a boutique feel, studios and apartments with fully equipped kitchens and balconies, weekly housekeeping, fitness center, on-site cafe, close to public transportation and nightlife.

6. Iasi Aparthotel:

- **Address:** Strada General Berthelot 31, Bucharest 010006, Romania

- **Phone:** +40 21 303 2900
- **Price Range:** $$ (Mid-range)
- **Highlights:** Central location near Victoriei Square, spacious and comfortable apartments with fully equipped kitchens and balconies, weekly housekeeping, 24-hour front desk, on-site restaurant, close to shops, museums, and attractions.

7. Carol Park Aparthotel:

- **Address:** Bulevardul Carol I 3-5, Bucharest 030167, Romania
- **Phone:** +40 21 319 0545
- **Price Range:** $ (Budget-friendly)
- **Highlights:** Family-friendly aparthotel in a picturesque location near Carol Park, studios and apartments with kitchenettes, playground, on-site cafe, close to green spaces and attractions, budget-friendly option with good value for money.

8. Old Town Residence Aparthotel:

- **Address:** Strada Lipscani 36, Bucharest 030002, Romania
- **Phone:** +40 733 056 928
- **Price Range:** $$ (Mid-range)
- **Highlights:** Charming aparthotel in the heart of Old Town, historic building with modern interiors, studios and apartments with fully equipped kitchens and balconies, daily housekeeping, 24-hour front desk, close to nightlife, restaurants, and attractions.

9. Romana Residence Aparthotel:

- **Address:** Piata Romana 5, Bucharest 010005, Romania
- **Phone:** +40 21 408 6800
- **Price Range:** $$ (Mid-range)
- **Highlights:** Stylish and modern aparthotel in a prestigious area near

Piata Romana, spacious and comfortable studios and apartments with kitchenettes, on-site laundry facilities, fitness center, rooftop terrace with city views, close to shops, cafes, and attractions.

10. Green Suites Herastrau Aparthotel:

- **Address:** Șoseaua Nordului 96-98, Bucharest 011370, Romania
- **Phone:** +40 21 310 3800
- **Price Range:** $$ (Mid-range)
- **Highlights:** Peaceful location near Herastrau Park and Lake, studios and apartments with fully equipped kitchens and balconies, private gardens or terraces available, children's playground, on-site restaurant, close to green spaces and recreational activities.

- 6 Historic Mansions in Bucharest

Here are 6 of the most captivating historic mansions in Bucharest:

1. Cantacuzene Palace:

- **Address:** Strada I.C. Brătianu 2, Bucharest 030167, Romania
- **Description:** This majestic neoclassical palace, built in the early 1900s for Prince Grigore Cantacuzene, is a masterpiece of architectural grandeur. Its imposing facade, adorned with intricate statues and carvings, tells a story of wealth and power. Today, the palace houses the Museum of Art Collections, showcasing an impressive collection of Romanian and

international art.

2. Știrbey Palace:

- **Address:** Strada Dr. Iuliu Barasch 28, Bucharest 011924, Romania
- **Description:** This stunning Art Nouveau gem, commissioned by Prince Barbu Știrbey in 1897, is a captivating blend of French and Romanian architectural styles. Its elegant facade, featuring wrought-iron balconies and stained glass windows, exudes a sense of timeless beauty. Currently, the palace serves as the Museum of the City of Bucharest, offering a fascinating journey through the city's history.

3. Ghika Palace:

- **Address:** Strada C.A. Rosetti 18-20, Bucharest 010005, Romania
- **Description:** This opulent Neo-Renaissance palace, built in the late 19th century for Prince Grigore Ghika, is a symbol of Bucharest's Belle Époque era. Its intricate decoration, featuring sculpted reliefs and ornate balconies, reflects the refined taste of its former residents. Today, the palace houses the Museum of Romanian Literature, preserving the literary heritage of the nation.

4. Bellu Mansion:

- **Address:** Strada Dr. Nicolae Kretzulescu 30, Bucharest 010003, Romania
- **Description:** This charming neoclassical mansion, built in the early 19th century for the Bellu family, is a haven of architectural elegance. Its symmetrical facade, with its wrought-iron balconies and delicate columns, exudes a sense of tranquility. Currently, the mansion houses the National Institute of Monuments, safeguarding Romania's cultural treasures.

5. Crețulescu Palace:

- **Address:** Strada Lipscani 36, Bucharest 030002, Romania
- **Description:** This historic mansion, built in the early 19th century by the wealthy merchant Nicolae Crețulescu, is a fascinating example of Ottoman-inspired architecture. Its unique blend of oriental and European elements, featuring colorful decorations and arched windows, tells a story of cultural exchange and artistic fusion. Today, the palace houses the Museum of the Romanian Peasant, showcasing the country's rich folk traditions.

6. Cesianu Racoviță Palace:

- **Address:** Strada Biserica Enei 16, Bucharest 030002, Romania
- **Description:** This exquisite palace, built in the 18th century for the Cantacuzino family, is a prime example of Brancoveanu architecture, named after Prince Constantin Brancoveanu. Its elaborate facade, adorned with intricate carvings and geometric patterns, reflects the artistic spirit of the era. Today, the palace houses the National Museum of George Enescu, celebrating the life and work of Romania's renowned composer.

- 7 Castles and Cottages in Bucharest

Here are 7 captivating options to consider for your trip, each offering a unique blend of history, beauty, and rural charm:

1. Mogoșoaia Palace:

- **Address:** Șoseaua București-Ploiești 99, Mogoșoaia, Ilfov, Romania
- **Phone:** +40 21 408 2345
- **Description:** This stunning 17th-century palace, nestled amidst lush gardens, is a prime example of Brancoveanu architecture. Its intricate carvings, elegant towers, and serene lakeside setting create a fairytale-like atmosphere. Explore the palace's richly decorated interiors, wander through the expansive gardens, and soak in the tranquility of the surrounding nature.

2. Știrbey Castle:

- **Address:** Șoseaua București-Ploiești 97, Buftea, Ilfov, Romania
- **Phone:** +40 722 299 222
- **Description:** This magnificent Neo-Gothic castle, built in the early 20th century for Prince Barbu Știrbey, is a testament to opulence and grandeur. Its imposing towers, stained glass windows, and spacious halls whisper tales of aristocratic life. Tour the castle's lavish interiors, admire the stunning stained glass windows, and explore the picturesque park surrounding the property.

3. Cantacuzene Castle:

- **Address:** Strada Florica 2, Floreasca, Bucharest, Romania
- **Phone:** +40 766 252 525
- **Description:** This charming 19th-century castle, built by Prince Mihail Cantacuzene, boasts a unique blend of architectural styles. Its asymmetrical facade, colorful towers, and manicured gardens exude a playful and whimsical atmosphere. Today, the castle houses a luxurious hotel, offering guests a taste of aristocratic living.

4. Roșu Villa:

- **Address:** Strada Roșu 1, Snagov, Ilfov, Romania

- **Phone:** +40 722 289 666
- **Description:** This historic villa, built in the early 20th century for the Roşu family, is a prime example of Art Nouveau architecture. Its elegant facade, featuring intricate floral motifs and stained glass windows, reflects the artistic spirit of the era. Today, the villa houses a charming restaurant, offering guests a delightful dining experience in a beautiful setting.

5. Bran Cottage:

- **Address:** Strada Bran 14, Bran, Braşov, Romania
- **Phone:** +40 745 717 722
- **Description:** This rustic cottage, nestled in the picturesque Bran village, offers a glimpse into the traditional Romanian countryside. Its wooden walls, thatched roof, and cozy interiors create a warm and inviting atmosphere. Enjoy a delicious meal in the cottage's restaurant, explore the surrounding Bran Castle (Dracula's Castle), and soak in the breathtaking mountain scenery.

6. Şerban Vodă Monastery:

- **Address:** Strada Mănăstirea Şerban Vodă 1, Târgovişte, Dâmboviţa, Romania
- **Phone:** +40 371 422 311
- **Description:** This historic monastery, founded in the 17th century by Prince Şerban Vodă, is a masterpiece of Wallachian architecture. Its imposing walls, ornate frescoes, and peaceful gardens offer a haven of spiritual serenity. Explore the monastery's church and museum, admire the stunning Byzantine-inspired architecture, and find tranquility amidst the surrounding nature.

7. Hanu' lui Manuc:

- **Address:** Strada Ştefan cel Mare 15, Câmpulung Muscel, Argeş, Romania

- **Phone:** +40 248 512 540
- **Description:** This traditional inn, built in the 18th century, is a living testament to Romanian history and culture. Its wooden walls, carved ceilings, and cozy atmosphere transport you back in time. Enjoy a delicious meal in the inn's restaurant, listen to traditional music, and soak in the authentic Romanian ambiance.

- Glamping Places in Bucharest

Here are 10 top glamping places near Bucharest, each offering a unique blend of nature, comfort, and adventure:

1. La Nucet Eco Resort:

- **Address:** DN10 km 88, Pietroșani, Ilfov 077190, Romania
- **Phone:** +40 729 259 073
- **Price Range:** $$ (Mid-range)
- **Highlights:** Nestled among the rolling hills of Snagov Lake, La Nucet Eco Resort offers luxurious safari-style tents with private bathrooms, balconies, and stunning lake views. Enjoy kayaking, hiking, cycling, and horseback riding in the scenic surroundings. On-site restaurant serves delicious organic fare.

2. Green Sheep Glamping:

- **Address:** Șoseaua București-Ploiești 97, Buftea, Ilfov 077125, Romania

- **Phone:** +40 726 796 796
- **Price Range:** $$$ (Luxury)
- **Highlights:** Located within the Știrbey Castle estate, Green Sheep Glamping provides stylish bell tents with plush bedding, private bathrooms, and wood-burning stoves for added coziness. Guests can enjoy horseback riding lessons, archery, and nature walks in the beautiful park surroundings.

3. Tentsile Treehouses at Corbeanca Lake:

- **Address:** Lacul Corbeanca, Șoseaua Corbeanca-Pantelimon, Ilfov 077190, Romania
- **Phone:** +40 724 869 252
- **Price Range:** $ (Budget-friendly)
- **Highlights:** Experience a truly unique stay suspended amongst the trees in these eco-friendly tentsile treehouses. Each cozy unit comes with comfortable beds, hammocks, and breathtaking lake views. Explore the surrounding forest trails, go for a swim in the lake, or simply relax and enjoy the peaceful atmosphere.

4. La Ferma Glamping:

- **Address:** DJ101F km 7.5, Măgurele, Ilfov 077175, Romania
- **Phone:** +40 722 656 316
- **Price Range:** $$ (Mid-range)
- **Highlights:** La Ferma Glamping offers spacious and stylish bell tents equipped with comfortable beds, private bathrooms, and private terraces overlooking the surrounding farmland. Guests can enjoy horseback riding, farm tours, and traditional Romanian meals prepared with fresh local ingredients.

5. Paradisul Verde Glamping:

- **Address:** Șoseaua Alexandriei km 15, Tunari, Ilfov 077195, Romania

- **Phone:** +40 723 156 861
- **Price Range:** $$ (Mid-range)
- **Highlights:** Located near Tunari Lake, Paradisul Verde Glamping provides comfortable geodomes with panoramic windows, private bathrooms, and terraces for stargazing. Guests can enjoy swimming, fishing, and kayaking in the lake, or explore the nearby forests and meadows.

6. White Tent Resort:

- **Address:** Strada Șoseaua Gherghița 80-82, Snagov, Ilfov 077190, Romania
- **Phone:** +40 722 333 084
- **Price Range:** $$ (Mid-range)
- **Highlights:** White Tent Resort offers a luxurious glamping experience with stylish safari tents featuring plush bedding, private bathrooms, and hot tubs on private decks. Guests can enjoy boat trips on Snagov Lake, relax in the on-site spa, or savor delicious meals at the resort's restaurant.

7. La Moara Glamping:

- **Address:** DN71 km 58.5, Breaza, Prahova 105500, Romania
- **Phone:** +40 729 305 398
- **Price Range:** $$ (Mid-range)
- **Highlights:** La Moara Glamping offers a rustic glamping experience in cozy wooden cabins nestled among the hills near Breaza. Each cabin comes with comfortable beds, private bathrooms.

8. Valea Verde Glamping:

- **Address:** Șoseaua București-Ploiești 62, Corbeanca, Ilfov 077190, Romania
- **Phone:** +40 728 347 820
- **Price Range:** $$ (Mid-range)

- **Highlights:** Valea Verde Glamping offers spacious and colorful geodomes equipped with comfortable beds, private bathrooms, and panoramic windows overlooking the surrounding valley. Guests can enjoy hiking, bike riding, and ziplining in the nearby forest, or simply relax on the hammocks and soak in the serene atmosphere.

9. Conacul Alb Glamping:

- **Address:** Strada Pădurea Verde 8, Ştefăneştii de Jos, Ilfov 077190, Romania
- **Phone:** +40 742 189 384
- **Price Range:** $$ (Mid-range)
- **Highlights:** Conacul Alb Glamping provides a unique glamping experience in stylish safari tents decorated with traditional Romanian textiles. Each tent comes with comfortable beds, private bathrooms, and private terraces overlooking the picturesque grounds. Guests can enjoy horseback riding, archery, and traditional Romanian music evenings around the campfire.

10. Castelul de Lut Glamping:

- **Address:** DJ101F km 8.5, Măgurele, Ilfov 077175, Romania
- **Phone:** +40 722 690 863
- **Price Range:** $$ (Mid-range)
- **Highlights:** Castelul de Lut Glamping offers a fairytale-like escape in cozy hobbit-style houses made from natural materials. Each house comes with comfortable beds, private bathrooms, and wood-burning stoves for added warmth. Guests can enjoy swimming in the on-site lake, exploring the surrounding countryside, or participating in pottery workshops hosted by the glamping site.

5

Chapter 5

Exploring the Attractions

Palace of Parliament

Palace of Parliament

T he Palace of Parliament in Bucharest, also known as the House of the People, is a truly impressive and historically significant landmark. Here's the information of the Palace of Parliament:

- **Address:** Strada Izvorul 1-3, Bucharest 050011, Romania
- **Phone Number:** +40 21 311 3611

Operation Hours:

- **Standard Tours:** Monday to Sunday, 09:00 - 17:00 (last admission at 16:00)
- **Underground Tour (limited availability):** Only on Saturdays and Sundays, 10:00 and 15:00 (limited to 20 people per tour)

Fees:

- **Standard Tour:**Adults: 60 lei (approximately €12.50)
- Students (19-26 years old with valid ID): 30 lei (approximately €6.25)
- Children (7-18 years old): 20 lei (approximately €4.20)
- **Underground Tour:**Adults: 65 lei (approximately €13.50)
- Students (19-26 years old with valid ID): 35 lei (approximately €7.35)
- Children (7-18 years old): 25 lei (approximately €5.20)

Other details:

- **Free admission:** Children under 7 years old, people with disabilities with a valid card and their companion, tour guides (groups of minimum 10 adults).
- **Reservations:** Bookings for 1 to 9 people can be made only by phone, 24 hours prior to the visit, between 09:00 and 16:00. Bookings for groups of 10 people + can be made by email at least 3 days prior to the visiting date.
- **Valid identification:** Access is permitted only with a valid national identity card (ID card or passport).

- **Website:** http://cic.cdep.ro/ro/vizitare/programe-si-tarife-de-vizitare

Additional notes:

- The Palace of Parliament offers various types of tours, including the standard tour, the underground tour, and private tours.
- The standard tour lasts about 45 minutes and takes you through some of the most impressive halls and rooms of the palace.
- The underground tour is available on limited days and times and requires prior booking. It takes you through the hidden bunkers and tunnels beneath the palace.
- The Palace of Parliament is a popular tourist destination, so it is advisable to book your tour in advance, especially during peak season.

Old Town

Lipscani

Bucharest's Old Town, also known as Lipscani, pulsates with the city's vibrant past and present. Steeped in centuries of history, it offers a tapestry of cobbled streets, colorful buildings, and an energetic atmosphere that's sure to captivate you. Let's delve into its history, explore some fun activities, and find the easiest way to get there:

Lipscani

A Journey Through Time:

- **Medieval Beginnings:** Founded in the 14th century as a merchant settlement, Lipscani witnessed Bucharest's transformation from a small trading post to a bustling city. The name itself hints at its past, derived from "Lipsca," the German city of Leipzig, referencing the trade route that connected the two.
- **Turbulent Times:** The Old Town endured fires, earthquakes, and invasions, each leaving its mark on the architectural patchwork. Ottoman influences mingle with neoclassical elegance, and hidden courtyards whisper tales of resilience.
- **Cultural Crossroads:** Today, Lipscani is a melting pot of Romanian traditions and contemporary life. Artists showcase their talents, street performers entertain, and the air buzzes with the aroma of local delicacies.

Activities to Ignite Your Senses:

- **Embrace History:** Step back in time at the Curtea Veche (Old Princely Court), where rulers once resided. Marvel at the intricate carvings of Stavropoleos Church, the oldest in Bucharest, or explore the Hanul lui Manuc, a historic caravanserai transformed into a charming museum.
- **Indulge Your Taste Buds:** Embark on a culinary adventure through charming cafes and traditional restaurants. Sample hearty stews, savor delicious pastries, and sip on aromatic Romanian coffee. Don't miss the vibrant Viktualienmarkt, where fresh produce and local specialties tempt your palate.
- **Unleash Your Inner Shopaholic:** Browse through quaint handicraft shops bursting with colorful ceramics, hand-painted wooden treasures, and intricate embroidery. Discover unique art galleries and hidden boutiques selling contemporary Romanian designs.
- **Immerse Yourself in Culture:** Catch a captivating performance at the National Theatre, or lose yourself in the world of art at the National Museum of Romanian Art. Immerse yourself in live music at a pub or

dance the night away at a lively club.

Finding Your Way to Lipscani:

- **Walking Wonder:** The best way to experience the Old Town is on foot. Get lost in the labyrinthine streets, discover hidden gems, and soak in the captivating atmosphere. Comfortable shoes are your key companions on this cobblestone adventure.
- **Public Transport:** Buses and the metro offer convenient connections to Lipscani. The Piata Universitatii and Piata Romana stations are just a short walk away.
- **Taxis and Ridesharing:** Taxis and ridesharing apps like Uber are readily available and provide a comfortable option, especially with luggage.

Tips for the Best Experience:

- **Bring cash:** While many places accept cards, some smaller shops and vendors might prefer cash.
- **Learn some basic Romanian phrases:** A few key words go a long way in enhancing your interactions with locals.
- **Be aware of pickpockets:** As with any crowded tourist destination, take necessary precautions to keep your valuables safe.
- **Relax and enjoy:** Let the magic of Lipscani wash over you. Savor the sights, sounds, and smells, and create lasting memories in this timeless Bucharest treasure.

Whether you're a history buff, a foodie, or simply seeking a vibrant atmosphere, Bucharest's Old Town promises an unforgettable experience. So, lace up your shoes, grab your curiosity, and prepare to be enchanted by the charm of Lipscani!

Ateneul Român

Ateneul Român

The Ateneul Român, Bucharest's prestigious concert hall, offers a beautiful architectural gem and a vibrant hub for classical music lovers. Here's all you need to know:

- **Address:** Strada George Enescu 1-3, București 010005, Romania
- **Phone Number:** +40 21 315 2567
- **Website:** https://www.fge.org.ro/

Operation Hours:

- **Box Office:** Monday-Friday 10:00 - 18:00, Saturday-Sunday 10:00 - 13:00
- **Building Open for Guided Tours:** Monday-Friday 10:00 - 12:00 and 14:00 - 17:00

Fees:

- **Ticket Prices:** Vary depending on the concert or event. Check the website for specific details.
- **Guided Tour:** Adults – 30 lei (~€6.50), Students – 15 lei (~€3.25), Children (7–18) – 10 lei (~€2.20)

Fun Activities:

- **Attend a Concert:** Immerse yourself in the stunning acoustics and atmosphere of the Ateneul Român by attending a classical music concert. The George Enescu Philharmonic Orchestra regularly performs here, featuring local and international musicians.
- **Take a Guided Tour:** Discover the fascinating history and architectural details of the building through a guided tour. Learn about its construction, design inspirations, and role in Romanian cultural life.
- **Admire the Foyer:** Explore the grand foyer, featuring intricate stained glass windows, sculpted columns, and elegant marble stairs. Soak in the breathtaking ambience and imagine the elegant balls and events once held here.
- **Visit the Museum:** The building houses a small museum showcasing the history of the Ateneul Român and its connection to Romanian composer George Enescu. See historical instruments, photographs, and documents that trace the evolution of this cultural landmark.
- **Relax in the Gardens:** Enjoy a peaceful respite in the surrounding gardens. Stroll through the paths adorned with statues and fountains, and soak in the tranquility amidst the bustling city.

Other Necessary Details:

- **Dress code:** While there's no formal dress code, smart casual attire is recommended for concerts and tours.
- **Accessibility:** The building is wheelchair accessible.
- **Photography:** Allowed for personal use but not during concerts or events.
- **Food and Beverage:** A cafe is available in the building.

Tip: Check the Ateneul Român website for upcoming events and ticket information. Tickets can be purchased online or at the box office.

The National Museum of Art of Romania

The National Museum of Art of Romania

The National Museum of Art of Romania (MNAR) is a treasure trove of Romanian and international art, waiting to be discovered. Here's the information you need for your visit:

- **Address:** Strada Ion Câmpineanu 6-8, București 010005, Romania
- **Phone Number:** +40 21 312 0949
- **Website:** https://mnar.ro/

The interior

Operation Hours:

- Tuesday–Sunday: 10:00 – 18:00 (last admission at 17:30)
- Closed on Mondays, public holidays, and specific maintenance days.

Fees:

- **General Admission:** Adults – 50 lei (~€10.50), Students (19–26 years old with valid ID) – 25 lei (~€5.25), Children (7–18 years old) – 10 lei (~€2.10), Children under 7 – Free.
- **Temporary Exhibitions:** Additional fees may apply for special exhibitions. Check the website for details.
- **Free admission:** Every first Friday of the month (except June, July, and August), International Museum Day (May 18), and Culture Day (November 30).

How to Get There:

- **Public Transportation:** The MNAR is conveniently located near Piata

Revolutiei and can be reached by metro (Universitate or Piata Romana stations) or by bus (lines 28, 301, 601, 605).

- **Taxis and Ridesharing:** Taxis and ridesharing apps like Uber are readily available and offer a comfortable option, especially with luggage.
- **Walking:** For those enjoying a stroll, the MNAR is within a 15-minute walk from Piata Universitatii or a 20-minute walk from Piata Romana.

Fun Activities and Other Details:

- **Explore the Permanent Collection:** Immerse yourself in Romanian art from medieval icons and sculptures to 19th-century paintings and contemporary works. The museum houses an impressive collection covering various styles and periods.
- **Discover Temporary Exhibitions:** The MNAR regularly hosts diverse temporary exhibitions featuring international and Romanian artists. Check the website for current schedules.
- **Join a Guided Tour:** Gain deeper insights into the museum's collections and history by joining a guided tour, available in Romanian and English.
- **Enjoy the Atmosphere:** Relax in the beautiful courtyard or browse the museum shop for unique souvenirs.
- **Accessibility:** The MNAR is wheelchair accessible with elevators and ramps available.
- **Photography:** Allowed for personal use in designated areas with a photography permit.

Tips:

- Purchase tickets online in advance to avoid queuing, especially during peak season.
- Consider the "Museum Pass" for unlimited access to the MNAR and other museums for a year.
- Wear comfortable shoes, as the museum is quite large.
- Check the website for current information about exhibitions, events, and

closures.

Herăstrau Park

Herăstrau Park

Herăstrau Park, also known as King Michael I Park, is a sprawling green haven in the heart of Bucharest. With its glistening lake, verdant pathways, and diverse attractions, it's a must-visit for anyone seeking nature, recreation, or cultural immersion.

Herăstrau Park

Here's everything you need to know to plan your perfect Herăstrau Park adventure:

- **Address:** Strada Şoseaua Pavel D. Kiseleff 32, Bucureşti 011701, Romania
- **Phone Number:** +40 21 224 5860 (Administration office)
- **Operation Hours:** The park is open 24/7, but some attractions have specific opening hours.
- **Fees:** Free entry to the park itself. Individual attractions and activities may have separate fees.

Fun Activities:

- **Lake Adventures:** Rent a pedal boat, kayak, or swan paddle boat and explore the serene waters of Lake Herăstrau.
- **Cycling and Rollerblading:** Glide through the park's dedicated paths, enjoying the fresh air and scenic surroundings.
- **Picnic Paradise:** Spread out a blanket under the shade of a tree and enjoy a delightful picnic with friends or family.
- **Village Museum:** Immerse yourself in Romanian traditions at the charming Village Museum, showcasing traditional houses, crafts, and exhibits.

- **Japanese Garden:** Find tranquility and beauty in the serene Japanese Garden, featuring koi ponds, bridges, and meticulous landscaping.
- **Skate Park and Sports Facilities:** Get your adrenaline pumping at the skate park or enjoy a game of tennis, basketball, or volleyball on the designated courts.
- **Museum of Geology:** Explore the wonders of earth science at the Museum of Geology, featuring rock formations, fossils, and interactive exhibits.
- **Theater and Open-Air Events:** Catch a performance at the open-air theater or enjoy various seasonal events throughout the year.
- **Dining and Cafes:** Refuel after your park adventures at one of the many cafes and restaurants scattered throughout the park.

Other Necessary Details:

- **Accessibility:** The park is largely wheelchair accessible, with paved paths and ramps.
- **Restrooms:** Public restrooms are available throughout the park.
- **Picnic Areas:** Designated picnic areas with tables and benches are available.
- **Pets:** Dogs are allowed on leashes in specific areas of the park.
- **Safety:** The park is generally safe, but be aware of your surroundings and valuables.

Tips:

- Visit during the spring or autumn for the most pleasant weather and vibrant scenery.
- Wear comfortable shoes for walking and exploring the park.
- Bring sunscreen and a hat if visiting during the summer months.
- Rent a bike or a boat for a unique perspective of the park.
- Pack a picnic lunch or snacks to enjoy in the park.

No matter your interests, Herăstrau Park offers something for everyone. So, lace up your shoes, grab your camera, and prepare to be enchanted by this verdant oasis in the heart of Bucharest!

Grigore Antipa National Museum of Natural History

The interior

The Grigore Antipa National Museum of Natural History in Bucharest is a treasure trove for nature lovers, showcasing Romania's incredible biodiversity and the wonders of the natural world. Here's everything you need to know to plan your visit:

- **Address:** Pavel Dimitrievici Kiseleff Road no. 1, Bucharest 011701, Romania
- **Phone Number:** +40 21 312 0588

- **Website:** https://antipa.ro/

The interior

Opening Hours:

- Tuesday – Sunday: 10:00 AM – 6:00 PM
- Closed on Mondays, January 1, Easter Sunday, and December 25.

Fees:

- Adults: 30 lei (~€6.30)
- Students (19-26 years old with valid ID): 15 lei (~€3.15)
- Children (7-18 years old): 10 lei (~€2.10)
- Children under 7 years old: Free

Getting There:

- **Public Transportation:** The Antipa Museum is within walking distance of Piata Victoriei metro station. Buses 79, 93, and 136 also stop nearby.

- **Taxi or Ridesharing:** Taxis and ridesharing apps like Uber are readily available and offer a convenient option, especially with luggage.
- **Walking:** For those enjoying a stroll, the Antipa Museum is a pleasant 20-minute walk from Victoriei Square.

Fun Activities and Exhibits:

- **Explore Diverse Ecosystems:** Journey through dioramas showcasing Romania's various landscapes, from the Carpathian Mountains to the Black Sea coast.
- **Meet Fascinating Creatures:** Marvel at a vast collection of over 2 million specimens, including majestic mammals, colorful birds, and intriguing reptiles.
- **Discover Fossils and Minerals:** Travel back in time with dinosaur skeletons and prehistoric fossils, or admire the dazzling array of minerals and precious stones.
- **Interactive Exhibits:** Learn through play with interactive displays and educational activities, perfect for children and adults alike.
- **Temporary Exhibitions:** Catch exciting temporary exhibitions featuring specific themes or guest collections.

Other Necessities:

- **Accessibility:** The museum is wheelchair accessible with elevators and ramps available.
- **Photography:** Allowed for personal use in designated areas without flash.
- **Food and Beverage:** A cafe is located within the museum for refreshments.
- **Guided Tours:** English-language tours are available upon request for an additional fee.

Tips:

- Purchase tickets online in advance to avoid queuing, especially during peak season.
- Consider the "Museum Pass" for unlimited access to the Antipa Museum and other museums for a year.
- Wear comfortable shoes as the museum is quite large.
- Check the website for current information about temporary exhibitions, events, and closures.

With its impressive collections, interactive exhibits, and engaging atmosphere, the Grigore Antipa National Museum of Natural History promises a captivating journey into the wonders of the natural world. So, pack your curiosity and prepare to be amazed!

Snagov Monastery

Snagov Monastery, nestled on the picturesque Snagov Island in Bucharest's northern suburbs, offers a welcome respite from the city's bustle. This historic and serene monastery boasts centuries of rich history, stunning architecture, and a peaceful atmosphere perfect for reflection and spiritual exploration.

- **Address:** Strada Mănăstirii nr. 1, Snagov, Ilfov 077190, Romania
- **Phone Number:** +40 21 358 0025

Operation Hours:

- Church: Open daily from 8:00 AM to 6:00 PM.
- Monastery Grounds: Open daily from 7:00 AM to 7:00 PM.

Fees:

- Entrance to the church is free.
- Donations are welcome to support the monastery's upkeep.
- There is a small fee for photography within the church.

How to Get There:

- **By car:** The monastery is easily accessible by car, located about 18 km north of Bucharest city center. Follow signs for Snagov and the monastery.
- **By public transportation:** Take bus 301 from Piata Victoriei in Bucharest to Snagov village, then walk or take a taxi to the monastery.

Things to Do and See:

- **Explore the Church of the Holy Virgin:** This beautiful 16th-century church, adorned with intricate frescoes and carvings, is the monastery's centerpiece. Take in the serene atmosphere and admire the unique architectural style.
- **Visit the Princely Court:** The ruins of the former residence of Prince Vlad Dracul (father of Vlad the Impaler) offer a glimpse into the monastery's historical significance.
- **Wander the Monastery Grounds:** Stroll through the peaceful gardens and courtyards, surrounded by lush greenery and captivating views of Snagov Lake.
- **Attend a Church Service:** Immerse yourself in the spiritual atmosphere by attending a service in the church.
- **Enjoy a Traditional Meal:** Savor a delicious and authentic Romanian meal at the monastery's restaurant.

Other Important Details:

- Dress modestly when visiting the church and monastery grounds.

- Be respectful of the religious significance of the site.
- Photography is allowed within the church for a small fee.
- The monastery offers guided tours in Romanian and English for a deeper understanding of its history and significance.

Tips:

- Visit during the week to avoid weekend crowds.
- Wear comfortable shoes for walking around the monastery grounds.
- Bring a camera to capture the beauty of the monastery and its surroundings.
- Consider staying overnight at the monastery's guesthouse for a truly immersive experience.

Snagov Monastery promises a unique and enriching experience for anyone seeking a peaceful escape from the city, a journey through history, or a deeper connection to spirituality. So, pack your curiosity and prepare to be enchanted by this tranquil gem in the heart of Romania.

Arcul de Triumf

Arcul de Triumf

Bucharest's iconic Arcul de Triumf, standing tall and proud, welcomes you with its grand presence and rich history. Here's everything you need to know for a perfect visit:

- **Address:** Piața Arcul de Triumf, Bucharest 011725, Romania
- **Phone Number:** +40 21 312 0969 (Municipal Museum Administration)

Operation Hours:

- **Grounds:** Open daily 24/7.
- **Observation Deck (during climbing season):** Every weekend (Friday-Sunday) in June-October, from 10:00 AM to 6:00 PM. Tickets purchased on-site, first come, first served.

Fees:

- **Grounds:** Free access.
- **Observation Deck:** 10 lei (~€2.10) for adults, 5 lei (~€1.05) for children (7-14 years old), free for under 7 years.

Getting There:

- **Public Transportation:** Metro stations Victoriei (red line) or Piața Romană (blue line) are a short walk away. Several buses also stop nearby.
- **Taxi or Ridesharing:** Convenient options, especially with luggage.
- **Walking:** Enjoy a pleasant 20-minute walk from Piata Victoriei or a 30-minute walk from Piata Romană.

Things to Do:

- **Marvel at the Architecture:** Admire the triumphal arch's neoclassical design, featuring intricate reliefs and sculptures depicting Romania's victories in World War I.
- **Pose for Photos:** Capture iconic pictures under the majestic arch against the backdrop of Bucharest's skyline.
- **Climb the Observation Deck (seasonal):** Enjoy panoramic views of the city from the top of the 90-foot arch (limited availability, subject to season and weather).
- **Explore the Surrounding Area:** Stroll through the beautiful Kiseleff Park, visit the Știrbey Palace, or discover museums and restaurants nearby.

Other Necessary Details:

- **Accessibility:** The grounds are accessible by wheelchair, but the observation deck requires climbing stairs.
- **Restrooms:** Public restrooms are available near the arch.
- **Events:** The area around the arch frequently hosts concerts, festivals, and other events. Check local websites for schedules.

Tips:

- Visit during the day for the best light and views.
- Wear comfortable shoes for walking around the park.

- Check the weather forecast before climbing the observation deck, as strong winds might limit access.
- Consider a combination ticket with other museums for discounted entry.

With its historical significance, architectural beauty, and scenic location, Arcul de Triumf promises a memorable experience. So, lace up your shoes, grab your camera, and prepare to be captivated by this Bucharest landmark!

Stavropoleos Church in Bucharest

Stavropoleos Church

Stavropoleos Church (also known as Stavropoleos Monastery) is a breathtaking example of Brâncovenesc architecture, nestled in the heart of Bucharest's Old Town. Here's everything you need to plan your visit:

- **Address:** Strada Stavropoleos 4, București 030002, Romania
- **Phone Number:** +40 21 310 91 30
- **Website:** https://www.stavropoleos.ro/en/

The interior

Opening Hours:

- **Church:** Monday – Sunday, 9:00 AM – 5:00 PM (except during services)
- **Museum:** Tuesday – Sunday, 10:00 AM – 5:00 PM (closed on Mondays)

Admission Fees:

- **Church:** Free
- **Museum:** Adults: 15 RON; Students: 5 RON; Children under 7: Free

Other Necessary Details:

- **Photography:** Allowed in the church and the museum for a small fee.
- **Dress Code:** Modest attire is recommended.
- **Accessibility:** The church is accessible by stairs, but the museum has a wheelchair ramp.
- **Language:** Guided tours are available in Romanian, English, and French.

What to See and Do:

- **Marvel at the Brâncovenesc architecture:** The church boasts intricate stonework, decorative sculptures, and vibrant frescoes.
- **Explore the museum:** Learn about the history of the church and the Brâncovenesc style with exhibits and artifacts.
- **Attend a service:** Immerse yourself in the spiritual atmosphere of the church, which is still an active place of worship.
- **Relax in the courtyard:** Enjoy the peaceful ambiance of the inner courtyard, surrounded by the church's walls.

Tips:

- Book your tickets in advance for the museum, especially during peak season.
- Consider a guided tour to gain deeper insights into the church's history and architecture.
- Combine your visit with exploring the charming streets of Bucharest's Old Town.

Stavropoleos Church is a must-see for anyone visiting Bucharest. Its beauty, history, and spiritual significance make it a truly unique and unforgettable experience.

Cathedrals in Bucharest

However, there are two prominent cathedrals in Bucharest that you might be thinking of:

1. The National Cathedral of the Assumption of the Virgin Mary:

- **Address:** Calea Ștefan cel Mare 16, București 020003, Romania
- **Phone Number:** +40 21 317 79 10
- **Website:** https://catedrala-nationala.ro/
- **Opening Hours:**Church: Monday - Friday, 7:00 AM - 7:00 PM; Saturday & Sunday, 7:00 AM - 8:00 PM
- Crypt: Tuesday - Sunday, 10:00 AM - 4:00 PM
- **Admission Fees:** Free

Other Details:

- Photography allowed for personal use.
- Dress code: Modest attire recommended.
- Accessible by stairs, with limited wheelchair access.
- Guided tours available in Romanian and English (by request).

2. The Saint Joseph Roman Catholic Cathedral:

- **Address:** Str. Dealul Mitropoliei 15, București 030002, Romania
- **Phone Number:** +40 21 313 15 58
- **Website:** https://www.tripadvisor.com/Attraction_Review-g294458-d 12614156-Reviews-Saint_Joseph_Cathedral-Bucharest.html
- **Opening Hours:**Church: Monday - Friday, 9:00 AM - 12:00 PM & 3:00 PM - 6:00 PM; Saturday & Sunday, 8:00 AM - 1:00 PM & 4:00 PM - 8:00 PM
- **Admission Fees:** Free

Other Details:

- Photography allowed for personal use.
- Dress code: Modest attire recommended.
- Accessible by stairs.
- Guided tours available in Romanian and English (by request).

Both cathedrals are beautifully decorated and hold significant historical and cultural importance in Bucharest. Which one you choose to visit depends on your religious affiliation or personal preference.

The Museum of Art Collections

The interior

Bucharest's vibrant art scene offers a treasure trove for culture enthusiasts, and the Museum of Art Collections stands as a crown jewel amongst them. Nestled within the Romanit Palace on Calea Victoriei, this museum houses a diverse collection spanning Romanian and European art from the 19th and 20th centuries.

Here's everything you need to know to plan your visit:

- **Address:** Calea Victoriei 111, Sector 1, 010063 București, Romania
- **Phone Number:** +40 21 313 30 30
- **Website:** https://mnar.ro/

Opening Hours:

- Wednesday – Sunday: 10:00 AM – 6:00 PM
- Last entrance: 5:00 PM (Museum of Art Collections and National Museum of Art of Romania)
- Closed on Mondays, Tuesdays, and public holidays

Admission Fees:

- Adults: 15 RON (approximately 3.15 EUR)
- Seniors (over 65): 7 RON (approximately 1.45 EUR)
- Students: 5 RON (approximately 1.05 EUR)
- Children under 18: Free

Other Necessary Details:

- Photography is allowed for personal use without flash.
- Guided tours are available in Romanian and English (book in advance for groups).
- The museum is partially wheelchair accessible.
- A cloakroom is available for storing bulky items.

What to See and Do:

- Explore over 44 art collections showcasing Romanian and European paintings, sculptures, decorative arts, and more.
- Witness masterpieces by renowned Romanian artists like Theodor Aman, Nicolae Grigorescu, and Ioan Andreescu.
- Discover hidden gems of European art, including a drawing by Vincent van Gogh.
- Delve into the fascinating history of Romanian art through informative displays and curated exhibits.
- Immerse yourself in the opulent ambiance of the Romanit Palace, a masterpiece of Neoclassical architecture.

Must-See Collections:

- The Corneliu Baba Collection: Explore the expressive brushstrokes and bold colors of Romania's renowned Post-Expressionist artist.
- The Iosif Iser Collection: Discover the intriguing world of Surrealist and Symbolist art through Iser's captivating sculptures.
- The Marcu Beza - Hortensia and Vasile G. Beza Collection: Immerse yourself in the vibrant landscapes and captivating portraits of Romanian Modernism.

Tips:

- Combine your visit with the National Museum of Art of Romania, housed in the same building, for a comprehensive immersion in Romanian art.
- Check the museum's website for current temporary exhibitions and special events.
- Consider joining a guided tour for a deeper understanding of the artwork and the museum's history.
- Allow ample time to explore the vast collection and soak in the artistic atmosphere.

The Museum of Art Collections promises a journey through time and artistic styles, offering a glimpse into the soul of Romanian and European art. So, pack your curiosity and prepare to be captivated by the treasures within its walls!

ARCUB

The interior of ARCUB

ARCUB, the Bucharest Cultural Center, holds a vibrant pulse in the city's artistic heart. Situated on Lipscani Street 84-90, it serves as a platform for diverse cultural events, engaging exhibitions, and innovative projects, offering something for everyone.

Here's your ultimate guide to experiencing ARCUB:

- **Address:** Str. Lipscani nr. 84-90, București 030037
- **Phone Number:** +40 21 315 71 38
- **Website:** https://arcub.ro/

Opening Hours:

- **ARCUB – Hanul Gabroveni:** Tuesday - Sunday, 10:00 AM - 8:00 PM (closed on Mondays)
- **Casa Eliad:** Tuesday - Sunday, 10:00 AM - 6:00 PM (closed on Mondays)
- **Events:** Vary depending on the specific event

Admission Fees:

- **Exhibitions:** Varies depending on the specific exhibition; some are free while others have nominal fees.
- **Events:** Varies depending on the type of event; typically range from free to moderate prices.

Other Necessary Details:

- Photography is allowed for personal use without flash, except in specific cases where restrictions are noted.
- Guided tours are available for both ARCUB spaces (book in advance).
- Both spaces are partially wheelchair accessible.
- Cloakrooms are available for storing bulky items.

What to See and Do:

- Immerse yourself in diverse exhibitions covering visual arts, theatre, music, dance, and literature.
- Catch captivating performances, concerts, and theatrical productions

throughout the year.
- Attend engaging workshops, conferences, and educational programs on varied cultural topics.
- Explore the historic architecture of Hanul Gabroveni and Casa Eliad, former merchant houses transformed into artistic havens.
- Discover hidden gems in the charming Lipscani district, known for its vibrant energy and historical significance.

Current Highlights:

- **Universul lui Salvador Dalí:** Step into the surreal world of Salvador Dalí through this immersive exhibition until May 12, 2024.
- **Bucharest Jazz Festival:** Enjoy pulsating music and celebrate the spirit of jazz throughout November 2024.
- **Spotlight Festival:** Experience an urban light show illuminating Bucharest's iconic landmarks throughout October 2024.

Tips:

- Check ARCUB's website for a comprehensive calendar of events and exhibitions.
- Consider purchasing a multi-event pass for discounted access to multiple shows and exhibitions.
- Sign up for the ARCUB newsletter to stay updated on the latest cultural happenings.
- Combine your visit with exploring the nearby Lipscani district and its unique shops and cafes.

6

Chapter 6

Dining and Culinary Scene

- Local Cuisine and Specialties

Bucharest, the vibrant capital of Romania, tantalizes your taste buds with a delectable blend of local specialties and international influences. Embark on a culinary adventure through these 20 must-try dishes and drinks:

Savory Delights:

1: Sarmale: Tender cabbage leaves stuffed with seasoned minced meat, rice, and vegetables, simmered in a rich tomato sauce. A Romanian comfort food classic!

2: Tocană: Hearty stews, typically featuring pork, beef, or chicken, cooked with vegetables and spices like paprika and dill. Perfect for a chilly day.

3: Mici: Grilled skinless sausages seasoned with herbs and spices, often served with mustard and bread. A popular street food and a must-try for meat lovers.

4: Ciorbă: Sour soups with various bases like beef tripe, vegetables, or fish, often flavored with dill, lemon, and sour cream. A refreshing and flavorful option.

5: Polenta: A creamy porridge made from cornmeal, often served with cheese, stews, or fried onions. A versatile and comforting dish.

6: Gulyás: A Hungarian-inspired stew featuring beef, vegetables, and paprika. A hearty and flavorful option, especially popular in winter.

7: Varză à la Cluj: Braised cabbage with smoked meats and spices, a Transylvanian specialty with a smoky and savory flavor.

Sweet Indulgences:

8: Papanași: Fluffy doughnuts traditionally served with sour cream, jam, or fruit sauce. A light and sweet treat to end your meal.

9: Clătite: Thin pancakes traditionally filled with sweet or savory fillings like jam, cheese, or meat. A versatile option for breakfast, lunch, or a snack.

10: Cozonac: Sweet braided bread with raisins, nuts, or chocolate, often enjoyed during holidays like Easter and Christmas. A festive and delicious treat.

11: Halva: A dense and crumbly dessert made from sesame seeds, sugar, and sometimes nuts. A unique and flavorful option with a variety of textures.

Liquid Delights:

12: Țuică: A strong plum brandy, Romania's national drink. Enjoyed in small shots, often as an aperitif or digestif.

13: Vin de casă: Homemade wine, a popular choice among locals. Available in various red, white, and rosé varieties, offering a taste of local tradition.

14: Bere: Romanian beer, with a variety of brands and styles available. Craft breweries are also gaining popularity, offering unique and flavorful brews.

15: Cafea turcească: Turkish coffee, brewed strong and served in small cups. A traditional way to start your day or enjoy a quick caffeine boost.

Bonus Bites:

16: Salată de icre: A creamy salad made from carp roe, onions, and mayonnaise. A savory and flavorful appetizer.

17: Murături: Pickled vegetables, a common accompaniment to many Romanian dishes. Offers a tangy and refreshing counterpoint to rich flavors.

18: Gogoși: Deep-fried doughnuts, often served with powdered sugar or jam. A sweet and crispy treat perfect for a snack.

19: Placinta cu brânză: Pastries filled with cheese, a portable and delicious snack or light meal option. Available with various fillings and toppings.

20: Varză dulce: Sweet pickled cabbage, a unique and refreshing option. Offers a surprising twist on the classic pickled vegetables.

So, grab your appetite, venture beyond the familiar, and discover the vibrant flavors that await in this exciting city!

- Fine Dining Restaurants

Bucharest boasts a thriving fine dining scene, tantalizing gourmands with exquisite dishes, impeccable service, and elegant ambiance. Here are five top-notch restaurants to satisfy your cravings for a luxurious culinary experience:

1. JW Steakhouse: Indulge in prime cuts of steak cooked to perfection, paired with an extensive wine list and breathtaking views of the city from the 42nd floor of JW Marriott Bucharest Grand Hotel.

- **Address:** Calea Dorobanți 151, București 011701, Romania
- **Phone Number:** +40 21 300 5050
- **Operation Hours:** Tuesday-Sunday: 6:00 PM - 11:00 PM
- **Fees:** À la carte menu, expect prices around €60-€120 per person
- **Other Details:** Dress code: smart casual, reservations recommended

2. Joseph by Joseph Hadad: Embark on a culinary adventure through the Middle East at this Michelin-starred restaurant. Chef Joseph Hadad's creative interpretations of traditional dishes will tantalize your taste buds.

- **Address:** Strada George Enescu nr. 4, București 011922, Romania
- **Phone Number:** +40 733 049 748
- **Operation Hours:** Tuesday-Saturday: 6:00 PM - 11:30 PM
- **Fees:** Tasting menus from €85-€125, à la carte also available
- **Other Details:** Dress code: smart casual, reservations essential

3. Relais & Chateaux Le Bistrot Francais: Savor the timeless elegance of French cuisine in this exquisite setting. Expect fresh seasonal ingredients, impeccable service, and a wine cellar boasting over 500 labels.

- **Address:** Strada Nicolae Golescu 18, București 011701, Romania
- **Phone Number:** +40 756 018 393
- **Operation Hours:** Daily: 12:00 PM - 10:00 PM

- **Fees:** À la carte menu, expect prices around €50-€80 per person
- **Other Details:** Dress code: smart casual, reservations recommended

4. **Vacamuuu:** Experience a modern take on Romanian cuisine at this stylish restaurant. Chef Paul Ionescu reimagines traditional dishes with innovative techniques and seasonal ingredients, offering a truly delectable dining experience.

- **Address:** Șoseaua Pipera 45, Voluntari, Ilfov 077190, Romania
- **Phone Number:** +40 723 295 992
- **Operation Hours:** Tuesday-Saturday: 6:00 PM - 11:30 PM, Sunday: 12:00 PM - 4:00 PM
- **Fees:** Tasting menus from €75-€125, à la carte also available
- **Other Details:** Dress code: smart casual, reservations recommended

5. **L'Atelier Relais & Chateaux:** Immerse yourself in a sophisticated atmosphere at this Michelin-starred restaurant housed in a charming historical building. Chef Radu Dumitrescu's contemporary French cuisine, with a focus on local ingredients, promises an unforgettable culinary journey.

- **Address:** Intrarea Aurora 17C, București 011701, Romania
- **Phone Number:** +40 740 089 565
- **Operation Hours:** Monday-Saturday: 12:00 PM - 10:00 PM
- **Fees:** Tasting menus from €95-€145, à la carte also available
- **Other Details:** Dress code: smart casual, reservations essential

Beyond these highlights, Bucharest's fine dining scene offers a plethora of options to suit diverse palates and preferences. Be sure to research menus, dress codes, and reservation policies before embarking on your culinary adventure. Whether you crave classic French fare, innovative twists on Romanian cuisine, or a global fusion of flavors, Bucharest's fine dining scene promises an unforgettable gourmet experience.

- Budget-Friendly Eateries

Here are five budget-friendly eateries that promise amazing flavors without burning a hole in your pocket:

1. Hanu' Lui Manuc (Manuc's Inn): Step back in time at this historical caravanserai, now a bustling restaurant serving traditional Romanian fare. Savor hearty stews like ciorbă, grilled mici sausages, and polenta with cheese, all at incredibly affordable prices.

- **Address:** Strada Lipscani 58, București 010004, Romania
- **Phone Number:** +40 21 314 5479
- **Operation Hours:** Daily: 11:00 AM - 11:00 PM
- **Fees:** Main courses around €5-€10, budget-friendly set menus available
- **Other Details:** Cash only, lively atmosphere, perfect for experiencing local culture

2. La Mama Kitchen and Bar: Craving comfort food? This cozy eatery serves up generous portions of pasta, burgers, and hearty salads at reasonable prices. Their daily specials and lunchtime deals offer even more value, making it a perfect spot for a satisfying and affordable meal.

- **Address:** Strada Popa Sotirescu 19, București 010070, Romania
- **Phone Number:** +40 727 339 975
- **Operation Hours:** Monday-Friday: 11:00 AM - 11:00 PM, Saturday-Sunday: 10:00 AM - 11:00 PM
- **Fees:** Main courses around €7-€12, lunch deals and daily specials available
- **Other Details:** Debit/credit cards accepted, casual atmosphere, great for groups

3. Ciorbăria La Radu: Get your fill of authentic Romanian soups at this no-frills eatery. Choose from a variety of ciorbă, each brimming with vegetables and meat or fish, for a filling and flavorful meal. With prices starting around €3 for a bowl, it's the perfect budget-friendly lunch or dinner option.

- **Address:** Strada Gabroveni 8, București 010640, Romania
- **Phone Number:** +40 729 805 294
- **Operation Hours:** Monday-Friday: 8:00 AM - 6:00 PM, Saturday-Sunday: 9:00 AM - 3:00 PM
- **Fees:** Bowls of ciorbă from €3-€5, additional dishes like polenta and pickles also available
- **Other Details:** Cash only, simple and clean atmosphere, ideal for a quick and budget-friendly meal

4. Falafel Beirut: Immerse your taste buds in Middle Eastern delights at this popular street food stall. Their freshly made falafel wraps, packed with savory chickpeas, vegetables, and flavorful sauces, are a satisfying and affordable treat. Prices start at just €2 for a falafel wrap, making it perfect for a grab-and-go lunch or a light dinner.

- **Address:** Piața Romană 5, București 010541, Romania (and other locations)
- **Phone Number:** +40 728 856 725
- **Operation Hours:** Daily: 10:00 AM - 10:00 PM
- **Fees:** Falafel wraps from €2-€4, additional toppings available
- **Other Details:** Cash only, street food stall with limited seating, vegetarian and vegan options available

5. Sandwicheria Veche: Satisfy your cravings for classic Romanian street food at this beloved hole-in-the-wall sandwich shop. Their iconic "sandvisuri" are simple yet delicious, featuring crusty bread piled high with fresh ingredients like ham, cheese, vegetables, and pickles. Priced from just €1.50, they're a budget-friendly way to experience a local favorite.

- **Address:** Calea Victoriei 122, București 010005, Romania (and other locations)

- **Operation Hours:** Monday-Friday

7

Chapter 7

Shopping in Bucharest

- Shopping Districts

Whether you seek high-end fashion, handcrafted souvenirs, or everyday essentials, get ready to unleash your inner shopaholic and explore these alluring shopping havens:

1. Calea Victoriei: Bucharest's most elegant avenue, lined with grand 19th-century buildings. Indulge in luxury brands like Gucci, Dior, and Louis Vuitton, or browse art galleries and antique shops. Soak in the architectural grandeur and vibrant street life while you shop.

Things to sell: High-end fashion, art galleries, antique shops, jewelry stores, cafes, restaurants.

2. Dorobanți: Home to Bucharest's fashion elite, Dorobanți boasts designer boutiques, trendy concept stores, and chic cafes. Discover Romanian fashion labels alongside international brands, and find the perfect outfit for a night out on the town.

Things to sell: Fashion boutiques, concept stores, cafes, restaurants, beauty salons

3. Lipscani: Step back in time in Bucharest's historic old town, Lipscani. Cobblestone streets wind past colorful buildings housing souvenir shops, antique stores, and local artisan stalls. Find traditional crafts, hand-painted ceramics, and unique Romanian souvenirs.

Things to sell: Souvenirs, handicrafts, antiques, clothing, jewelry, cafes, restaurants

4. Floreasca: A modern district with a mix of high-end retail and everyday essentials. Shop for groceries at Mega Image supermarket, browse homeware stores like IKEA, or catch a movie at the multiplex cinema. Take a break at one of the cafes or restaurants after your shopping spree.

Things to sell: Supermarkets, homeware stores, electronics stores, clothing stores, cafes, restaurants, cinema

5. Obor Market: Experience the vibrant bustle of Bucharest's largest marketplace. Obor Market overflows with fresh produce, flowers, meats, and cheeses, alongside clothing, household goods, and local crafts. Immerse yourself in the lively atmosphere and bargain for the best deals.

Things to sell: Fresh produce, flowers, meat, cheese, clothing, household goods, crafts

Pro Tip: If you're a bargain hunter, visit Bucharest during the seasonal sales, typically held in July and January. Many stores offer significant discounts on clothing, electronics, and other goods.

Happy shopping in Bucharest! Remember to bring your bargaining skills and an empty suitcase to fill with treasures.

- Souvenirs and Unique Finds

Bucharest, the vibrant capital of Romania, is a treasure trove waiting to be unearthed. Beyond the charming architecture and rich history, the city offers a delightful array of souvenirs and unique finds to take home or gift to loved ones. Whether you seek traditional handicrafts, artistic creations, or quirky keepsakes, Bucharest has something for everyone.

Traditional Delights:

- **Handpainted ceramics:** Immerse yourself in the vibrant colors and intricate patterns of Romanian ceramics. From decorative plates and mugs to figurines and jewelry, these handcrafted pieces make for beautiful reminders of your trip.
- **Ia blouses:** The iconic Romanian blouse, or "ie," is a symbol of national pride and cultural heritage. Each region boasts its own unique style and embroidery, making each piece a true one-of-a-kind treasure.
- **Wooden handicrafts:** Discover the intricate woodwork of the Carpathian Mountains in decorative boxes, figurines, and even furniture. These traditional pieces add a touch of rustic charm to any home.

Artistic Expressions:

- **Modern art:** Bucharest's burgeoning art scene offers a plethora of unique artwork to choose from. Paintings, sculptures, and jewelry created by local artists make for meaningful souvenirs that support the creative community.
- **Vintage posters:** Travel back in time with vintage posters depicting Romanian landscapes, historical events, or cultural icons. These nostalgic pieces add a touch of character to any wall.
- **Handmade jewelry:** From delicate wire-wrapped pieces to bold statement necklaces, Bucharest's independent jewelry designers offer unique creations that will add a touch of personality to your outfit.

Quirky Keepsakes:

- **Palinca:** Romania's national drink, this strong plum brandy comes in various flavors and is a unique souvenir for those who enjoy a spirited tipple.
- **Communist memorabilia:** For history buffs, Bucharest offers a plethora of communist-era trinkets and souvenirs, from busts of Lenin to keychains adorned with the Romanian hammer and sickle.
- **Vinyl records:** Discover hidden gems at Bucharest's vintage record stores. From Romanian folk music to international classics, you're sure to find something to add to your collection.

Where to Find Your Treasures:

- **Lipscani:** Explore the maze of cobblestone streets in Bucharest's old town, overflowing with souvenir shops and artisan stalls.
- **Hanul lui Manuc:** Step back in time at this historic caravanserai, now home to a bustling marketplace offering traditional crafts and local delicacies.
- **Art galleries and independent shops:** Discover unique pieces and support local artists by browsing Bucharest's many art galleries and independent shops.
- **Floreasca market:** For a more eclectic experience, head to Floreasca market, where you'll find everything from antiques and clothing to fresh produce and handmade crafts.

Tips for Souvenir Savvy:

- **Haggling is expected:** In some markets, particularly Lipscani, haggling is part of the fun. Don't be afraid to negotiate for a better price!
- **Check the quality:** Ensure you're buying authentic handicrafts by checking for quality materials and craftsmanship.
- **Pack carefully:** Fragile items like ceramics or wooden handicrafts need

careful packing to ensure they arrive home safely.

· **Support local artists:** Choose souvenirs made by local artisans whenever possible to support the creative community and preserve Romanian traditions.

So, go forth and explore the hidden gems Bucharest has to offer! With its diverse array of souvenirs and unique finds, your trip will be filled with treasured memories and tangible pieces of Romanian culture to take home with you. Happy shopping!

8

Chapter 8

Nightlife and Entertainment

- Bars and Pubs

B ucharest's nightlife scene is a vibrant tapestry, woven from trendy cocktail bars to cozy pubs brimming with local character. Whether you're craving craft brews, innovative mixology, or a lively atmosphere, these five spots promise an unforgettable evening:

Bars:

1: **Baracca:** Tucked away in the historical Lipscani district, Baracca is a hidden gem oozing speakeasy vibes. Dimly lit and adorned with vintage decor, it offers an extensive cocktail menu featuring classics with a twist and experimental creations. Live jazz music on weekends adds to the speakeasy charm.

- **Address:** Strada Lipscani 42, București 010005, Romania
- **Phone Number:** +40 727 394 428
- **Operation Hours:** Tuesday–Sunday: 6:00 PM – 3:00 AM

- **Fees:** Cocktails around €10-€15
- **Other Details:** Cash only, reservations recommended

2: Ciuculet: Experience contemporary cocktail artistry at Ciuculet, a sleek bar hidden behind a vintage clothing store. Their talented bartenders craft innovative cocktails using seasonal ingredients and local spirits, pushing the boundaries of mixology. Expect an intimate and sophisticated atmosphere.

- **Address:** Strada Popa Sotirescu 15, București 010070, Romania
- **Phone Number:** +40 755 026 053
- **Operation Hours:** Tuesday-Saturday: 6:00 PM - 2:00 AM, Sunday: 6:00 PM - 12:00 AM
- **Fees:** Cocktails around €12-€15
- **Other Details:** Reservations recommended

3: The Social Club: For a touch of British flair, head to The Social Club. This lively bar boasts a vibrant atmosphere, friendly staff, and a wide selection of beers, cocktails, and pub grub. Catch live sports on the big screens or join in on their regular quiz nights and themed events.

- **Address:** Strada Șelari 9, București 010005, Romania
- **Phone Number:** +40 788 443 159
- **Operation Hours:** Monday-Sunday: 12:00 PM - 3:00 AM
- **Fees:** Beers from €5, cocktails from €8
- **Other Details:** No reservations, large groups welcome

4: Zero Zero: Immerse yourself in the cool and quirky setting of Zero Zero, a bar housed in a former communist-era cinema. Exposed brick walls, vintage furniture, and eclectic decor create a unique ambiance. Sip on creative cocktails or choose from their extensive selection of spirits and craft beers.

- **Address:** Strada Pictor Arthur Verona 16, București 010099, Romania
- **Phone Number:** +40 733 634 545

- **Operation Hours:** Tuesday-Sunday: 5:00 PM - 3:00 AM
- **Fees:** Cocktails around €10-€15
- **Other Details:** No reservations, cash preferred

5: Nomad Skybar: Breathtaking views await at Nomad Skybar, Bucharest's highest cocktail bar perched on the 11th floor of a modern hotel. Sip on signature cocktails while admiring panoramic cityscapes, especially stunning at sunset. Reservations are essential for securing a prime spot.

- **Address:** Calea Dorobanți 15-17, București 011701, Romania (Top Floor)
- **Phone Number:** +40 737 025 230
- **Operation Hours:** Sunday-Thursday: 4:00 PM - 1:00 AM, Friday-Saturday: 4:00 PM - 2:00 AM
- **Fees:** Cocktails around €15-€20
- **Other Details:** Reservations strongly recommended, dress code: smart casual

Pubs:

1: Caru' cu Bere: Step back in time at Caru' cu Bere, Bucharest's oldest beer hall. Housed in a stunning 19th-century building, it offers a traditional Bavarian atmosphere with live music, hearty food, and an extensive selection of local and international beers. Be prepared for a lively and bustling environment.

- **Address:** Stavropoleos 5 Street, Bucharest Old Town
- **Phone Number:** +40 726 282 373
- **Operation Hours:** Monday-Sunday: 9:00 AM - 12:00 AM
- **Fees:** À la carte menu, expect prices around €20-€30 per person (main courses)
- **Other Details**: Reservations recommended, live music most evenings, dress code: smart casual wear.

- Live Music Venues

Bucharest's nightlife pulsates with the rhythm of live music, offering a diverse soundscape for every taste. From intimate jazz bars to energetic rock clubs, the city provides a platform for both local and international talents. Here are five vibrant venues to ignite your musical wanderlust:

1. Control Club: A Bucharest institution, Control Club is a sprawling complex housing multiple spaces for live music, DJs, and dancing. Expect an eclectic mix of genres, from indie and alternative rock to electronic beats, all within a gritty and industrial setting. Catch renowned DJs or discover up-and-coming local bands in the various areas, each with its own unique vibe.

- **Address:** Strada Poiana Movilăţii 32-34, Bucureşti 077190, Romania
- **Phone Number:** +40 725 326 168
- **Operation Hours:** Vary depending on events, typically open late until 3:00 AM
- **Fees:** Cover charges vary depending on the event, ranging from €5-€20
- **Other Details:** Cash only, large and vibrant atmosphere, diverse range of music

2. Green Hours Jazz Club: Immerse yourself in the smoky allure of classic jazz at Green Hours. This intimate club, tucked away in the historic Lipscani district, features top-notch Romanian and international jazz musicians, captivating audiences with their improvisational flair. Savor a cocktail or a glass of wine in the dimly lit ambiance while losing yourself in the soothing melodies of trumpet, saxophone, and piano.

- **Address:** Strada Lipscani 45, Bucureşti 010005, Romania
- **Phone Number:** +40 723 632 913
- **Operation Hours:** Tuesday-Sunday: 8:00 PM - 3:00 AM
- **Fees:** Cover charges vary depending on the event, typically around €10-€15

- **Other Details:** Reservations recommended, intimate and atmospheric setting, focus on jazz music

3. Quantic Club: Quantic Club pulses with the energy of electronic music. This sleek and modern venue hosts renowned DJs from around the world, spinning sets that span house, techno, and everything in between. Immerse yourself in the vibrant dance floor atmosphere, fueled by pulsating bass lines and mesmerizing visuals. Quantic is the perfect place to let loose and groove until the early hours.

- **Address:** Strada Șelari 9, București 010005, Romania
- **Phone Number:** +40 722 559 520
- **Operation Hours:** Friday-Saturday: 11:00 PM - 5:00 AM
- **Fees:** Cover charges vary depending on the event, typically around €10-€20
- **Other Details:** No reservations, dress code: smart casual, focus on electronic music

4. La Scena Music Club: Experience the diversity of Bucharest's live music scene at La Scena. This versatile venue showcases an array of genres, from rock and pop to Balkan beats and acoustic singer-songwriters. The intimate setting fosters a close connection between artists and the audience, creating a truly immersive experience. Enjoy a casual drink or a bite to eat while discovering new musical talents or revisiting classic favorites.

- **Address:** Strada Șelari 13, București 010005, Romania
- **Phone Number:** +40 722 335 182
- **Operation Hours:** Wednesday-Sunday: 6:00 PM - 3:00 AM
- **Fees:** Cover charges vary depending on the event, typically around €5-€10
- **Other Details:** No reservations, casual atmosphere, diverse range of music

5. Sala Palatului: For a grand musical experience, step into the majestic Sala Palatului. This prestigious concert hall, designed in the Neo-Gothic style, hosts renowned orchestras, ballet performances, and classical concerts by international artists. The opulent setting and exceptional acoustics create an unforgettable atmosphere for appreciating musical masterpieces.

- **Address:** Strada Ion Voiavod 25, Bucureşti 011701, Romania
- **Phone Number:** +40 21 314 3378
- **Operation Hours:** Varies depending on events
- **Fees:** Ticket prices vary depending on the performance
- **Other Details:** Formal dress code for some events.

- Theatres and Performance Spaces

Bucharest's vibrant cultural scene comes alive on the stages of its diverse theatres and performance spaces. From historic landmarks to intimate studios, the city offers a feast for the senses, catering to every theatrical taste. Here are five captivating venues to explore:

1. National Theatre of Bucharest (I.L. Caragiale): Immerse yourself in the grandeur of Romanian theatre at the National Theatre. This imposing neoclassical building, opened in 1973, boasts six halls and an outdoor amphitheater, showcasing a comprehensive repertoire of classics, contemporary plays, and experimental productions. Witness the talent of renowned Romanian actors and directors in a setting steeped in cultural significance.

- **Address:** Bulevardul Nicolae Bălcescu 2, Bucureşti 010006, Romania
- **Phone Number:** +40 21 313 9175
- **Operation Hours:** Box office: Tuesday-Sunday 10:00 AM - 8:00 PM,

showtimes vary depending on the performance
- **Fees:** Ticket prices range from €5 - €30
- **Other Details:** Grand and historic setting, diverse repertoire, wheelchair accessible

2. Odeon Theatre: Experience the charm of a smaller, Art Nouveau theatre at the Odeon. Founded in 1946, this elegant venue presents intimate productions focusing on contemporary Romanian playwrights and innovative interpretations of classics. Its Sala Majestic, boasting plush red seats and ornate balconies, provides a cozy and theatrical atmosphere for enjoying captivating performances.

- **Address:** Calea Victoriei 40-42, București 010071, Romania
- **Phone Number:** +40 21 314 7394
- **Operation Hours:** Box office: Tuesday-Sunday 10:00 AM - 8:00 PM, showtimes vary depending on the performance
- **Fees:** Ticket prices range from €5 - €25
- **Other Details:** Art Nouveau architecture, intimate setting, focus on contemporary Romanian theatre

3. Act Theatre: Discover the avant-garde spirit of Bucharest at the Act Theatre. This independent venue established in 1990 champions experimental productions, bold interpretations of classics, and contemporary international works. Its intimate black-box setting fosters a close connection between performers and the audience, offering a platform for thought-provoking and challenging theatre experiences.

- **Address:** Calea Victoriei 126, București 010004, Romania
- **Phone Number:** +40 21 312 0613
- **Operation Hours:** Box office: Tuesday-Sunday 10:00 AM - 8:00 PM, showtimes vary depending on the performance
- **Fees:** Ticket prices range from €5 - €20
- **Other Details:** Independent and experimental theatre, intimate setting,

diverse repertoire

4. Podul Grant Theater: Embrace the charm of outdoor theatre at Podul Grant. Located in the heart of Herastrau Park, this open-air venue offers a unique experience under the summer sky. From children's plays and musicals to contemporary productions and classics, Podul Grant provides a refreshing and family-friendly way to enjoy theatre in a natural setting.

- **Address:** Parcul Herastrau, Bd. Aviatorilor, București 011802, Romania
- **Phone Number:** +40 728 156 793
- **Operation Hours:** Performances typically held during summer months, specific hours vary depending on the show
- **Fees:** Ticket prices range from €5 - €15
- **Other Details:** Open-air theatre in Herastrau Park, family-friendly atmosphere, seasonal performances

5. Green Hours Comedy Club: Laugh the night away at the Green Hours Comedy Club. This intimate venue in Lipscani district hosts stand-up comedians from Romania and around the world, delivering a dose of laughter and wit. Enjoy a drink and a bite to eat while soaking up the comedic energy and experiencing the vibrant atmosphere of Bucharest's underground comedy scene.

- **Address:** Strada Lipscani 45, București 010005, Romania
- **Phone Number:** +40 723 632 913
- **Operation Hours:** Shows typically Fridays and Saturdays at 8:00 PM, stand-up open mic on Wednesdays
- **Fees:** Entrance fee around €10-€15
- **Other Details:** Intimate comedy club, international and Romanian comedians, lively atmosphere.

9

Chapter 9

Day Trips and Nearby Destinations

Historical and Cultural Gems

Bran Castle

Bran Castle, also known as Dracula's Castle, is a captivating landmark nestled in the heart of Romania's Transylvanian Mountains. Its gothic silhouette evokes both awe and intrigue, drawing visitors from around the world eager to uncover its secrets. Delve into the history, explore the must-see attractions, and discover exciting activities to make your visit to Bran Castle a truly unforgettable experience:

History Unraveled:

- **14th Century:** The fortress was erected by the Teutonic Knights as a strategic point to defend against the Ottoman Empire.
- **Vlad the Impaler:** While not his primary residence, Vlad III Dracula (the inspiration for Bram Stoker's character) did use the castle during his reign in the 15th century as a temporary administrative center and rumored

prison.

- **Royal Residence:** From the late 19th century until the end of World War II, Bran Castle served as a summer residence for Romania's Queen Marie, who transformed it into a vibrant home filled with art and historical relics.
- **Modern Times:** Today, Bran Castle is a museum showcasing Queen Marie's collections, medieval artifacts, and furniture.

Must-See Attractions:

- **Grand Staircase:** Ascend the iconic oak staircase adorned with intricately carved coats of arms, leading you into the heart of the castle.
- **Queen Marie's Apartments:** Step into the Queen's lavishly decorated private chambers, filled with colorful tapestries, antiques, and personal belongings.
- **Throne Room:** Witness the grandeur of the Throne Room, adorned with stained glass windows and medieval weaponry.
- **Walk on the Walls:** Explore the narrow passageway along the castle's exterior walls, offering breathtaking views of the surrounding Carpathian Mountains.
- **Dracula's Crypt:** Descend into the dark and atmospheric crypt, rumored to be Vlad the Impaler's final resting place (although historically unproven).

Fun Activities:

- **Guided Tours:** Immerse yourself in the castle's history with a guided tour, offered in several languages and revealing fascinating insights into its past.
- **Costume Rentals:** Channel your inner prince or princess by renting period costumes and posing for photos within the castle walls.
- **Horse-Drawn Carriage Ride:** Travel back in time with a romantic horse-drawn carriage ride through the picturesque village below the castle.
- **Dracula Park:** Visit the nearby Dracula Park, an open-air museum featuring traditional houses, workshops, and live demonstrations of local

crafts and customs.

- **Hiking and Exploring:** Lace up your hiking boots and explore the surrounding mountains, discovering hidden waterfalls, stunning viewpoints,
and quaint villages.

Brasov

Nestled amidst the breathtaking Carpathian Mountains, Brasov is a city
brimming with history, charm, and breathtaking scenery. Founded in the
13th century by Teutonic Knights, it served as a crucial trade center and
stronghold, leaving a legacy of fortified walls, majestic Gothic architecture,
and vibrant cultural traditions. Let's delve into the captivating essence of
Brasov, exploring its rich history, must-see attractions, and exciting activities
to make your visit truly unforgettable:

A Journey Through Time:

- **13th Century:** Established by the Teutonic Knights as a defensive outpost,
Brasov flourished as a trade center and cultural hub.
- **Medieval Era:** The city witnessed the rise of powerful guilds, the construction of iconic landmarks like the Black Church and the Council Square,
and the reign of Vlad the Impaler (inspiration for Dracula).
- **Habsburg Rule:** Brasov came under Habsburg rule in the 17th century,
influencing its architecture and cultural landscape.
- **Modern Times:** Today, Brasov is a thriving tourism destination, celebrated for its medieval charm, rich history, and scenic natural surround-

ings.

Must-See Attractions:

- **The Black Church:** This towering Gothic masterpiece, named for a devastating fire in the 17th century, boasts impressive stained glass windows, intricate sculptures, and a haunting organ.
- **Council Square:** The heart of Brasov's Old Town, this lively square is surrounded by colorful buildings, bustling cafes, and street performers, offering a vibrant glimpse into city life.
- **Mount Tampa Cable Car:** Ascend the 960-meter mountain via the scenic cable car, enjoying panoramic views of the city and surrounding landscape. Hike among the trails or visit the Hollywood-inspired "Brasov" sign at the summit.
- **Bran Castle (Dracula's Castle):** While not directly in Brasov but a convenient day trip, this iconic landmark perched on a hilltop exudes Gothic charm and legends of Vlad the Impaler. Explore the Queen Marie's Apartments, walk on the ramparts, and delve into the myths surrounding Dracula.
- **Екатерининский парк (Catherine's Park)**: Escape the city bustle in this peaceful park, boasting lush greenery, walking paths, a charming lake, and the ruins of the Catherine Gate, offering a glimpse into Brasov's medieval fortifications.

Fun Activities:

- **Explore the Old Town:** Get lost in the maze of cobbled streets, discover hidden courtyards, and admire the architectural gems, from Baroque facades to colorful merchant houses.
- **Sample Local Delicacies:** Indulge in hearty Romanian cuisine like sarmale (stuffed cabbage leaves), polenta with cheese, and gulaş (stew). Don't miss the delicious pastries and locally-crafted beers.
- **Go Hiking:** Lace up your boots and explore the surrounding Carpathian

Mountains, discover hidden waterfalls, trek through lush forests, and enjoy breathtaking panoramas.

- **Visit nearby Castles:** Apart from Bran Castle, venture to the majestic Peles Castle, a Neo-Renaissance masterpiece filled with opulent interiors and stunning gardens, or explore the imposing Rasnov Fortress perched on a hilltop.
- **Witness Traditional Crafts:** Immerse yourself in Brasov's rich cultural heritage by visiting workshops where artisans showcase traditional crafts like wood carving, blacksmithing, and lacemaking.

Sibiu

Nestled amidst rolling hills and picturesque landscapes, Sibiu is a vibrant city humming with rich history, architectural treasures, and captivating charm. Founded in the 12th century by Saxon settlers, it flourished as a trade center and cultural hub, leaving behind a legacy of grand squares, ornate buildings, and a unique blend of Saxon and Romanian traditions. Let's dive into the magic of Sibiu, exploring its captivating past, must-see attractions, and exciting activities that will make your visit truly unforgettable:

A Journey Through Time:

- **12th Century:** Founded by Saxon settlers as a fortified town, Sibiu thrived as a trade center and member of the Hanseatic League.
- **Medieval Era:** The city witnessed the construction of iconic landmarks

like the Council Tower, the Bridge of Lies, and the magnificent Lutheran Cathedral, reflecting its prosperity and artistic flair.

- **Habsburg Rule:** Sibiu came under Habsburg rule in the 17th century, influencing its architecture and cultural landscape, introducing Baroque elements and a cosmopolitan atmosphere.
- **Modern Times:** Today, Sibiu is a thriving cultural center and tourism destination, celebrated for its well-preserved Altstadt (Old Town), unique festivals, and lively artistic scene.

Must-See Attractions:

- **The Big Square:** The heart of Sibiu's Old Town, this vibrant square is lined with colorful Renaissance and Baroque buildings, bustling cafes, and lively street performers. Don't miss the imposing Brukenthal National Museum.
- **The Bridge of Lies:** This iconic covered bridge, adorned with intricate statues and rumored to reveal the truthfulness of anyone crossing it, is a must-see for its charming legend and breathtaking views.
- **The Council Tower:** Climb the 77-meter tower, the symbol of Sibiu, for panoramic vistas of the city and surrounding landscape. Explore the museum exhibits showcasing the city's history and cultural treasures.
- **The ASTRA National Museum of Traditional Village:** Immerse yourself in Romanian rural life at this open-air museum, featuring over 100 traditional houses from different regions, workshops showcasing crafts, and live demonstrations of folk traditions.
- **The Passage of Stairs:** Discover this hidden gem, a maze of covered stairways connecting the streets of the Upper Town, offering a unique perspective of the city and a touch of whimsical exploration.

Fun Activities:

- **Explore the Old Town:** Get lost in the labyrinthine streets, admire the architectural gems, and soak in the vibrant atmosphere. Discover hidden courtyards, unique shops, and charming cafes tucked away in corners.

- **Sample Local Delicacies:** Indulge in Sibiu's culinary delights, from hearty stews and polenta dishes to fresh salads and delectable pastries. Don't miss the local Transylvanian cheese and plum brandy.
- **Witness the Sibiu International Theatre Festival:** Experience the city's vibrant artistic scene during this renowned festival, featuring theatrical performances, workshops, and street artists.
- **Visit the Transylvanian Museum of Saxon Ethnography:** Immerse yourself in the rich cultural heritage of the Transylvanian Saxons at this museum, showcasing traditional costumes, furniture, and artifacts.
- **Day Trip to nearby Villages:** Discover the charm of Saxon villages like Cisnadioara and Talmaciu, featuring fortified churches, colorful houses, and traditional crafts.

Ruse, Bulgaria

Nestled on the banks of the mighty Danube River, Ruse is a vibrant Bulgarian city boasting a rich history, architectural treasures, and a captivating blend of cultures. Founded in the 7th century, it has witnessed the rise and fall of empires, leaving behind a legacy of Ottoman mosques, Roman ruins, and Neoclassical grandeur. Let's delve into the charm of Ruse, exploring its fascinating past, must-see attractions, and exciting activities that will make your visit truly unforgettable:

A Journey Through Time:

- **7th Century:** Founded as a Byzantine fortress named Sexaginta Prista, Ruse served as a strategic point on the Danube.
- **Ottoman Era:** From the 14th to the 19th century, Ruse flourished under Ottoman rule, becoming a major trade center and cultural hub. This era left behind a legacy of mosques, baths, and Ottoman architecture.
- **Liberation and Modern Times:** After gaining independence in 1878, Ruse emerged as an important industrial center and cultural hub, experiencing a period of rapid development. Today, it is a vibrant city known for its historical charm, lively artistic scene, and welcoming atmosphere.

Must-See Attractions:

- **The Danube River:** The lifeblood of Ruse, the Danube offers breathtaking views, boat trips, and a tranquil escape from the city bustle. Take a cruise, enjoy a picnic on the banks, or simply admire the majestic river flowing past.
- **Sveta Troitsa Church:** This magnificent Neo-Byzantine church, adorned with colorful mosaics and intricate frescoes, is a masterpiece of religious architecture and an iconic landmark of Ruse.
- **The Pantheon of National Revival Heroes:** Pay your respects at this impressive mausoleum honoring Bulgarian heroes who fought for the country's independence. Explore the museum exhibits showcasing their stories and contributions.
- **Ruse Regional Museum of History:** Delve into the rich history of Ruse at this museum, housing archaeological finds, artifacts from different eras, and exhibits showcasing the city's development.
- **Monument to Freedom:** Climb the steps to this imposing monument offering panoramic views of the city and commemorating the liberation of Ruse from Ottoman rule.

Fun Activities:

- **Explore the Old Town:** Get lost in the charming maze of cobbled streets, discover hidden courtyards, and admire the architectural gems, from Ottoman mosques to Neoclassical buildings.

- **Sample Local Delicacies:** Indulge in the flavors of Bulgarian cuisine, from hearty stews and grilled meats to fresh salads and delicious pastries. Don't miss the local Tarator soup and yogurt drinks.
- **Enjoy the Art Scene:** Immerse yourself in Ruse's vibrant art scene, visit galleries showcasing contemporary works, and attend live music performances or theater shows.
- **Take a Day Trip to Ivanovo Rock Churches:** Explore the UNESCO-listed Ivanovo Rock Churches, carved into the cliffs near Ruse and boasting medieval frescoes and stunning views.
- **Relax in the Parks:** Escape the city bustle and soak in the tranquility of Ruse's parks, like the Garden of the Virgin Mary or the Borisova Garden, offering greenery, walking paths, and cafes for a refreshing break.

Nature and Adventure

Piatra Craiului National Park

Nestled in the heart of the Făgăraș Mountains of Romania, Piatra Craiului National Park encompasses a breathtaking landscape of soaring limestone ridges, lush forests, and emerald grasslands. Its name, meaning "King's Rock," hints at the majestic presence of the Piatra Craiului Massif, which dominates the park with its dramatic cliffs and jagged peaks.

A Walk Through Time:

- **Geological Origins:** Millions of years of erosion sculpted the distinctive limestone karst landscape, shaping caves, gorges, and the iconic ridge that forms the park's backbone.
- **Human History:** Evidence of human presence dates back to the Paleolithic era, with traces of Dacian and Roman settlements further showcasing the area's rich past.
- **National Park Status:** Established in 1973, Piatra Craiului National Park protects over 14,700 hectares of biodiversity and scenic beauty.

Must-See Attractions:

- **The Piatra Craiului Ridge:** Hike or climb along the park's iconic limestone ridge, enjoying panoramic views and encountering challenging yet rewarding terrain.
- **Zărnești Gorges:** Explore the dramatic Zărnești Gorges, carved by glaciers and rivers, featuring waterfalls, caves, and diverse flora and fauna.
- **Plaiul Foii Meadow:** Discover a haven of wildflowers and panoramic vistas at Plaiul Foii Meadow, ideal for picnics and enjoying the serene mountain atmosphere.
- **Curmătura Refuge:** Rest and refuel at the cozy Curmătura Refuge, situated at the foot of the Piatra Craiului Ridge, offering stunning views and traditional Romanian cuisine.
- **Șaua Zăplațului Cave:** Embark on a spelunking adventure in the impressive Șaua Zăplațului Cave, adorned with stalactites and stalagmites, and featuring an underground waterfall.

Fun Activities:

- **Hiking and Climbing:** Lace up your boots and explore the park's extensive network of trails, catering to all levels of experience, from gentle forest paths to challenging climbs on the Piatra Craiului Ridge.

- **Wildlife Watching:** Keep your eyes peeled for the park's diverse wildlife, including chamois, wild boars, deer, eagles, and numerous bird species.
- **Photography:** Capture the breathtaking scenery, dramatic rock formations, and vibrant flora and fauna through your lens.
- **Picnicking and Relaxing:** Find a serene spot amongst the meadows and forests, enjoy a picnic with breathtaking views, and soak in the tranquility of nature.
- **Traditional Village Visits:** Discover the charm of nearby villages like Zărneşti and Peştera, experiencing local culture, handicrafts, and delicious home-cooked meals.

Essential Information:

- **Address:** Parcul National Piatra Craiului, Str. Victoriei 72, Zărneşti 50550, Romania
- **Phone Number:** +40 269 555 049
- **Operation Hours:** The park is open year-round, but access to certain areas like the Piatra Craiului Ridge may be restricted due to weather conditions.
- **Fees:** Entrance fees vary depending on the season and activities. Hiking trails are generally free, while cave visits and climbing permits require fees.
- **Other Details:** Comfortable footwear, proper clothing for changing weather conditions, and sun protection are recommended. Be sure to pack enough water and snacks for your activities.

Moieciu

Moieciu, nestled amidst the breathtaking Făgăraş Mountains of Romania, is not just a charming village but a gateway to a wonderland of natural beauty, historical treasures, and outdoor adventures. Its name whispers of ancient whispers, echoing through time from the Dacians who once called this valley home. Let's delve into the heart of Moieciu, exploring its captivating history, must-see attractions, and exciting activities that will make your visit truly unforgettable:

A Journey Through Time:

- **Dacian Origins:** Moieciu's lands were inhabited by the Dacians, a fierce Thracian tribe, who left behind traces of their presence in archaeological sites like the Piatra Craiului National Park.
- **Medieval Era:** The area flourished under the rule of the Transylvanian Saxons, who established villages and introduced their architectural style and cultural traditions.
- **Modern Times:** Today, Moieciu is a thriving tourist destination, celebrated for its stunning scenery, traditional villages, and proximity to the Piatra Craiului National Park.

Must-See Attractions:

- **Castelul Bran (Dracula's Castle):** While not directly in Moieciu, this iconic landmark perched on a hilltop near Braşov is a must-visit for its Gothic charm and legends of Vlad the Impaler. Explore the Queen Marie's Apartments, walk on the ramparts, and delve into the myths surrounding Dracula.
- **Piatra Craiului National Park:** Embark on an adventure in this breathtaking park, featuring the iconic Piatra Craiului Ridge, lush forests, Zărneşti Gorges, and diverse flora and fauna. Hike, climb, relax in meadows, and witness the park's natural wonders.

- **Moieciu de Sus and Moieciu de Jos:** Explore these charming villages, discover traditional houses, wooden churches, and the warmth of local hospitality. Sample delicious home-cooked meals and immerse yourself in the authentic Romanian village atmosphere.
- **Ruginoasa Waterfall:** Witness the cascading beauty of Ruginoasa Waterfall, hidden amidst the lush forest. Take a refreshing dip in the cool waters or enjoy a picnic by the falls.
- **Peștera Liliecilor (Cave of Bats):** Embark on a spelunking adventure in this unique cave, home to a colony of bats. Explore the cave formations, discover hidden chambers, and learn about the fascinating world of bats.

Fun Activities:

- **Hiking and Climbing:** Lace up your boots and explore the extensive network of trails in the Piatra Craiului National Park, catering to all levels of experience. Hike through forests, climb the challenging Piatra Craiului Ridge, or simply enjoy leisurely walks with stunning views.
- **Mountain Biking:** Embark on thrilling bike rides through the scenic trails of the Făgăraș Mountains. Discover hidden valleys, conquer challenging climbs, and enjoy the adrenaline rush of mountain biking.
- **Horseback Riding:** Explore the Moieciu Valley on horseback, enjoying the unique perspective and connection with nature. Choose from gentle rides through meadows to adventurous trails in the mountains.
- **Wildlife Watching:** Keep your eyes peeled for the diverse wildlife of the area, including chamois, deer, eagles, and numerous bird species. Capture their beauty with your camera or simply enjoy the sight of these majestic creatures in their natural habitat.
- **Traditional Crafts and Food:** Immerse yourself in the rich cultural heritage of Moieciu. Visit local artisans showcasing their skills in wood carving, pottery, and weaving. Sample traditional Romanian dishes like sarmale (stuffed cabbage leaves), polenta with cheese, and delicious pastries.

Bucharest Delta

Bucharest Delta, also known as Văcărești Nature Park, is a captivating green haven nestled amidst the bustling streets of Romania's capital city. This urban oasis boasts a fascinating history, diverse flora and fauna, and a wealth of opportunities for outdoor recreation and relaxation. Let's dive into the wonders of Bucharest Delta, exploring its intriguing past, must-see attractions, and exciting activities that will make your visit truly unforgettable:

A Journey Through Time:

- **19th Century:** The area initially served as a royal hunting ground and later housed a monastery, which was unfortunately demolished in the 1980s to make way for a reservoir project that was never completed.
- **1986-1989:** During the communist era, construction began on a massive reservoir, but the project was abandoned due to economic and environmental concerns.
- **1990s-Present:** Over time, the abandoned construction site transformed into a vibrant natural ecosystem, becoming a refuge for numerous plant and animal species. In 2014, it was officially declared a protected area known as Văcărești Nature Park.

Must-See Attractions:

- **Wetlands and Lakes:** Embrace the calming atmosphere of the Delta's wetlands and lakes, home to diverse aquatic plants, birds, and insects. Witness the reflection of the city skyline on the lake's surface and enjoy the tranquility of nature.
- **Observatory Platform:** Climb the wooden observation platform and soak in panoramic views of the entire Delta, encompassing the lush greenery, winding waterways, and the distant cityscape.
- **Woodland Trails:** Lace up your walking shoes and explore the network

of trails meandering through the Delta's woodlands. Discover hidden meadows, encounter diverse plant and animal species, and breathe in the fresh air.

- **Biodiversity:** Keep your eyes peeled for the Delta's rich biodiversity, including over 200 species of birds, reptiles, amphibians, and mammals. Spot majestic herons, listen to the melodious song of warblers, and maybe even catch a glimpse of a shy fox or deer.
- **Open-Air Museum:** Discover the remnants of the abandoned construction project, now transformed into an open-air museum. Explore the concrete structures, learn about the history of the area, and find creative ways to interact with the space.

Fun Activities:

- **Birdwatching:** Grab your binoculars and embark on a birdwatching adventure. Identify different species, capture their beauty with your camera, and learn about their crucial role in the Delta's ecosystem.
- **Picnics and Relaxation:** Find a peaceful spot amongst the trees or by the lake and enjoy a picnic with friends and family. Soak in the sunshine, breathe the fresh air, and disconnect from the city's hustle and bustle.
- **Cycling and Jogging:** Explore the Delta on two wheels or on foot. Cycle along the designated paths, jog through the trails, and immerse yourself in the natural surroundings.
- **Volunteer Opportunities:** Contribute to the preservation of this urban oasis by participating in volunteer activities organized by the park. Help with clean-up initiatives, plant trees, and raise awareness about the importance of the Delta.
- **Cultural Events:** Throughout the year, the Delta hosts various cultural events, from open-air concerts and art exhibitions to educational workshops and festivals. Check the park's schedule to see what coincides with your visit.

10

Chapter 10

Practical Tips

- Language and Communication

Bucharest, the vibrant capital of Romania, boasts a rich and complex linguistic landscape. Understanding the language and communication dynamics can greatly enhance your experience in this captivating city. Here's a dive into the intricacies of Bucharest's language scene:

Dominant Language:

- **Romanian:** Spoken by the vast majority of the population, Romanian is the official language of Bucharest and all of Romania. It belongs to the Romance language family, sharing similarities with Italian, French, and Spanish.

Foreign Language Penetration:

- **English:** While not an official language, English enjoys widespread understanding and usage, especially in the tourism and business sectors. Many younger generations and individuals working in service industries possess varying degrees of English proficiency.

- **French and Spanish:** Traces of these Romance languages linger due to historical and cultural influences. Some older generations or individuals from specific professions might be more comfortable in these languages.
- **Russian:** Due to historical ties, some elderly residents or individuals with Russian backgrounds might speak Russian.

Communication Tips:

- **Learning Basic Romanian Phrases:** Mastering essential greetings, polite expressions, and simple directions can go a long way. Learning the Cyrillic alphabet used for written Romanian might also be helpful.
- **Gestures and Body Language:** Romanians often use expressive gestures and body language to emphasize their communication. Familiarity with some common gestures can aid understanding.
- **Patience and Openness:** Embrace the possibility of language barriers as a potential challenge and opportunity to connect through non-verbal cues and a smile.
- **Seek Assistance:** Don't hesitate to ask for help from locals when needed. Many Romanians are eager to assist foreign visitors, and even those with limited English will make an effort to help you find your way.

Additional Information:

- **English Signage:** Major tourist attractions, hotels, and restaurants often have English signage and menus.
- **Translation Apps:** Utilize mobile translation apps for on-the-go assistance with understanding signs, menus, or conversing with locals.
- **Cultural Sensitivity:** Be mindful of cultural differences in communication styles. Romanians tend to be more direct and assertive than some cultures, but also value politeness and respect.

Beyond Languages: Bucharest embraces a diverse and multicultural atmosphere. Immerse yourself in the city's artistic energy, vibrant nightlife, and rich historical tapestry. Be open to experiencing communication beyond words, through gestures, music, and the shared human experience.

By understanding the language dynamics and embracing the cultural landscape, you can navigate Bucharest with confidence and connect with its welcoming people. So, pack your curiosity, a little Romanian, and a big smile, and prepare to be charmed by this fascinating city!

- Currency and Payment

When it comes to currency and payment in Bucharest, let's untangle the threads and ensure you navigate the financial scene smoothly:

Official Currency:

- **Romanian Leu (RON):** Bucharest, and all of Romania, uses the Romanian Leu (RON) as its official currency. You'll see prices displayed in RON and hear locals discussing amounts in "lei."

Payment Options:

- **Cash:** Although Romania increasingly embraces cashless transactions, carrying some RON in cash remains useful for smaller purchases at independent shops, street vendors, or public transportation tickets. ATMs dispensing RON are widely available throughout the city.

- **Credit Cards:** Most major credit cards like Visa, Mastercard, and American Express are widely accepted in hotels, restaurants, and larger shops. However, smaller establishments might only accept cash.
- **Debit Cards:** Debit cards with Maestro or VPay logos are generally accepted at ATMs and point-of-sale terminals. Check with your bank about any applicable fees for international transactions.
- **Contactless Payments:** Contactless payments through cards or mobile wallets are gaining popularity in Bucharest, especially in larger stores and chain establishments.

Things to Remember:

- **Exchanging Currency:** While you can exchange major currencies like Euros or USD at banks and authorized exchange offices, bringing some RON beforehand might be convenient for immediate needs. Comparing exchange rates before exchanging is recommended.
- **Tipping:** In Bucharest, tipping is not mandatory but customary in restaurants and certain service settings. A 10-15% gratuity is generally appreciated.
- **Scams:** Be cautious of currency exchange scams, especially on the streets. Opt for official exchange offices or reliable banks.
- **Foreign Transaction Fees:** Check with your bank about any potential foreign transaction fees associated with using your card abroad.

Pro Tip: Consider getting a "Wise Borderless Account" or similar service if you plan on spending significant amounts in RON. This allows you to hold multiple currencies at a cheaper exchange rate and avoid bank fees on international transactions.

- Safety Considerations and Local Etiquette

Bucharest, like any major city, has its charms and challenges. To ensure a safe and enjoyable experience, here are some safety considerations and local etiquette tips to keep in mind:

Safety:

- **General Precautions:** Stay alert in crowded areas, especially around tourist attractions and public transportation. Keep your valuables secure, avoid displaying expensive items, and be wary of pickpockets.
- **Nightlife:** Choose reputable bars and clubs in well-lit areas. Avoid wandering alone in deserted areas at night. If unsure, ask your hotel staff or locals for recommendations.
- **Public Transportation:** Validate your tickets on public transportation and be aware of your surroundings. Pickpocketing can occur, especially during peak hours.
- **Scams:** Beware of common scams like the "broken taxi meter" or the "gold ring trick." Stick to licensed taxis and avoid engaging with strangers offering unsolicited deals.
- **Emergency Numbers:** Dial 112 for emergencies (ambulance, police, fire).

Local Etiquette:

- **Greetings:** A handshake and a nod are common greetings. When addressing elders or people in positions of authority, use titles like "Mr." or "Mrs." followed by their last name.
- **Dining:** It's customary to wait to be seated and to dress modestly, especially in fine-dining establishments. Tipping is appreciated, usually around 10-15% of the bill.
- **Smoking:** Smoking is banned in most indoor public spaces, including restaurants and bars. Designated smoking areas might be available.
- **Public Behavior:** Avoid loud talking or public displays of affection.

Respect queuing and personal space in crowded areas.

- **Dress Code:** While casual attire is generally acceptable, avoid overly revealing clothing in religious or historical sites. Dress modestly when visiting churches or monasteries.

Additional Tips:

- Learn basic Romanian phrases for courtesy and asking for directions. Locals appreciate the effort to communicate in their language.
- Purchase a Bucharest City Card for discounted entry to museums, public transportation, and other attractions.
- Familiarize yourself with local customs and traditions to avoid unintentional disrespect.
- Trust your instincts and avoid situations that feel unsafe.

By following these tips and remaining vigilant, you can maximize your safety and enjoy Bucharest's vibrant culture and hospitality. Remember, respect goes a long way!

Have a wonderful and safe trip to Bucharest!

11

Chapter 11

Itinerary Ideas

- 14 Days of Family Fun in Bucharest

Bucharest, Romania's bustling capital, offers a captivating blend of history, culture, and outdoor adventures, making it an ideal destination for a family vacation. With 14 days to explore, you can create unforgettable memories for everyone, from exploring majestic castles to relaxing in serene parks. Here's a suggested itinerary:

Days 1-3: Unveiling the City's Charm:

- **Day 1:** Start your adventure with a stroll through the charming Old Town, admiring colorful houses, exploring hidden courtyards, and indulging in delicious street food. Visit the Palace of Parliament, one of the world's largest buildings, and marvel at its grandeur.
- **Day 2:** Embark on a treasure hunt at the National Museum of Natural History, where dinosaurs, rocks, and fascinating exhibits spark children's imagination. Climb the Triumph Arch for panoramic city views and take a funicular ride up Parliament Hill.

- **Day 3:** Step back in time at the Romanian Village Museum, an open-air museum showcasing traditional houses, crafts, and folk art. Enjoy a horse-drawn carriage ride, visit the zoo, and let the kids run free in Herastrau Park, Bucharest's green oasis.

Days 4-6: Beyond the City Walls:

- **Day 4:** Pack a picnic basket and head to Bran Castle, perched atop a hill and shrouded in Dracula's legend. Explore the castle's chambers, discover its history, and let the kids dress up as knights and princesses.
- **Day 5:** Take a day trip to Braşov, a medieval gem nestled in the Făgăraş Mountains. Climb Mount Tampa for breathtaking views, visit the Black Church, and explore the vibrant Piata Sfatului (Council Square).
- **Day 6:** Immerse yourselves in the natural beauty of Piatra Craiului National Park. Hike scenic trails, climb the challenging Piatra Craiului Ridge (suitable for older children), or explore the Zărneşti Gorges with its waterfalls and caves.

Days 7-9: Experiencing Local Treasures:

- **Day 7:** Dive into the world of science and technology at the Antipa Museum, home to dinosaurs, interactive exhibits, and a planetarium. Take a boat trip on the Danube River, offering stunning cityscapes and a unique perspective.
- **Day 8:** Learn about Romanian traditions at the Dimitrie Gusti National Village Museum, featuring a beautiful collection of traditional peasant houses and household items. Attend a folk dance performance or participate in a pottery workshop.
- **Day 9:** Get creative at the Theodor Aman Museum, housed in a charming neoclassical villa. Explore the artist's studio, admire his paintings and sculptures, and let the kids participate in art workshops.

Days 10-12: Fun and Relaxation:

- **Day 10:** Spend a thrilling day at Therme Bucharest, a massive water park with slides, pools, wave machines, and lazy rivers. Let the kids loose in the play areas while you unwind in the saunas and steam rooms.
- **Day 11:** Get active at Bucharest's many public parks and gardens. Play frisbee in Carol Park, rent a bike in Cişmigiu Park, or enjoy a picnic in Kiseleff Park with its lake and boat rentals.
- **Day 12:** Experience the magic of the circus at the Bucharest Circus, with acrobatic performances, clowns, and dazzling costumes. Alternatively, catch a family-friendly movie at one of the city's cinemas.

Days 13-14: Sweet Endings and Lasting Memories:

- **Day 13:** Indulge your sweet tooth at Bucharest's numerous cafes and pastry shops. Sample traditional Romanian desserts like "papanasi" (fried dough balls) and "cozonaci" (sweet bread), and enjoy the vibrant atmosphere.
- **Day 14:** Say goodbye to Bucharest with a final stroll through your favorite spots or discover something new. Reflect on the memories you

- Adventure Seeker's Guide

Bucharest, Romania's energetic capital, pulsates with hidden gems and adrenaline-pumping activities waiting to be discovered. Ditch the tourist traps and embark on a 14-day adventure designed for thrill seekers, nature enthusiasts, and history buffs. Get ready to explore subterranean caves, conquer challenging hikes, and unravel the city's mysteries – Bucharest awaits!

Days 1-3: Urban Spelunking and Hidden Histories:

- **Day 1:** Descend into the depths of Bucharest's underbelly with a guided tour of the Antipa Museum's Cave Hall. Marvel at stalactites and stalagmites sculpted by time, and discover fossils and hidden chambers in this subterranean wonderland.
- **Day 2:** Delve into Bucharest's secret past with a "Haunted Bucharest" tour. Explore eerie tunnels, abandoned buildings, and forgotten graveyards while listening to chilling tales of ghosts, vampires, and historical intrigue.
- **Day 3:** Embrace the city's artistic spirit with a street art and graffiti tour. Wander through colorful neighborhoods like Floreasca and Drumul Taberei, admiring murals, stencils, and hidden messages adorning walls and buildings.

Days 4-6: Nature's Playground and Outdoor Thrills:

- **Day 4:** Escape the city and head to Piatra Craiului National Park, a paradise for hikers and climbers. Scale the iconic Piatra Craiului Ridge for breathtaking panoramas, explore hidden waterfalls in Zărnești Gorges, or conquer challenging via ferratas.
- **Day 5:** Embark on a white-water rafting adventure on the Ialomița River, slicing through lush valleys and navigating rapids with friends and family. Enjoy the thrill of the water and soak in the scenic beauty of the surrounding countryside.
- **Day 6:** Get your adrenaline pumping at Therme Bucharest, a massive water park complex boasting thrilling slides, wave pools, and lazy rivers. Take on the "Free Fall" waterslide, test your nerve in the "Black Hole," or simply relax in the saunas and steam rooms.

Days 7-9: Historical Enigmas and Unexpected Delights:

- **Day 7:** Journey to Bran Castle, perched atop a hill and shrouded in

Dracula's legend. Explore the castle's chambers, discover its fascinating history, and unleash your inner vampire hunter while wandering through secret passageways.

- **Day 8:** Unravel the mysteries of the Romanian Athenaeum, a neoclassical gem known for its stunning architecture and acoustics. Take a guided tour, attend a classical music concert, or simply marvel at the intricate details of this cultural landmark.
- **Day 9:** Step back in time at the Village Museum, an open-air haven showcasing traditional Romanian houses, crafts, and folk art. Witness demonstrations of pottery making, wood carving, and blacksmithing, and soak in the atmosphere of a bygone era.

Days 10-12: Culinary Delights and Local Experiences:

- **Day 10:** Embark on a culinary adventure through Bucharest's vibrant food scene. Sample hearty stews like sarmale (stuffed cabbage leaves) and polenta with cheese at a traditional restaurant, indulge in decadent pastries at a local cafe, and explore bustling food markets.
- **Day 11:** Immerse yourself in the city's nightlife at one of Bucharest's trendy bars or clubs. From live music venues to rooftop terraces, the options are endless. Dance the night away, mingle with locals, and experience the city's energetic pulse.
- **Day 12:** Take a leisurely bike ride through Herastrau Park, the city's green oasis. Rent a boat and paddle on the lake, have a picnic under the trees, or simply relax and people-watch on the sunny lawns.

Days 13-14: Farewell Bucharest and Beyond:

- **Day 13:** Take a final stroll through your favorite spots, visit any museums you missed, or pick up souvenirs at the Piata Obor wholesale market. Reflect on the adventures you've had and the memories you've made.
- **Day 14:** Bid farewell to Bucharest

- 6 Days of Relaxation and Wellness in Bucharest

Bucharest, Romania's vibrant capital, might not be the first place that comes to mind for a wellness retreat. But beyond the bustling streets and lively nightlife, a haven of tranquility awaits. Embark on a 6-day journey designed to nourish your body, mind, and soul, leaving you feeling refreshed and revitalized.

Day 1: Setting the Tone for Tranquility

- **Morning:** Begin your day with a gentle yoga session in Carol Park, surrounded by lush greenery and fresh air. Breathe deeply, stretch your body, and set your intention for a week of well-being.
- **Afternoon:** Pamper yourself at Therme Bucharest, a sprawling water park complex. Float in the warm thermal pools, indulge in a rejuvenating massage, or relax in the saunas and steam rooms.
- **Evening:** Savor a delicious and healthy dinner at a vegetarian or vegan restaurant, like Rawcca or Shukran. Nourish your body with fresh, local ingredients and enjoy the peaceful atmosphere.

Day 2: Nature's Embrace and Inner Balance

- **Morning:** Immerse yourself in the serenity of Herastrau Park, Bucharest's green oasis. Rent a boat and paddle on the lake, take a leisurely bike ride on the designated paths, or simply have a picnic under the shade of the trees.
- **Afternoon:** Unwind and reconnect with nature at the Alexandru Ioan Cuza Botanical Garden. Wander through the serene gardens, discover diverse plant life, and breathe in the fresh air.
- **Evening:** Treat yourself to a traditional Romanian spa experience at the Baile Felix SPA. Soak in the mineral-rich thermal waters, enjoy mud treatments, and experience the healing power of nature.

Day 3: Cultural Delights and Culinary Delights

- **Morning:** Visit the Cantacuzene Palace, a stunning neoclassical gem nestled in Bucharest's charming Old Town. Admire the architectural details, explore the museum exhibits, and enjoy the peaceful atmosphere.
- **Afternoon:** Embark on a culinary adventure through Bucharest's vibrant food scene. Discover hidden gems serving traditional Romanian dishes like sarmale (stuffed cabbage leaves) and polenta with cheese, or indulge in international cuisine at trendy restaurants.
- **Evening:** Attend a classical music concert at the Romanian Athenaeum, a majestic concert hall renowned for its acoustics. Let the music wash over you as you relax and immerse yourself in the cultural experience.

Day 4: Inner Harmony and Creative Expression

- **Morning:** Find your inner balance through a meditation session at one of Bucharest's yoga studios, like Modo Yoga or Infinite Yoga. Disconnect from the outside world, focus on your breath, and cultivate inner peace.
- **Afternoon:** Unleash your creativity at the National Museum of Art of Romania. Wander through the extensive collection of paintings, sculptures, and decorative arts, and find inspiration in the works of Romanian and international masters.
- **Evening:** Enjoy a relaxing evening at a traditional Hammam, like the Kervansaray Hammam. Steam away your stress, get a traditional Turkish massage, and experience the ancient ritual of cleansing and renewal.

Day 5: Exploring Beyond the City Walls

- **Day Trip:** Escape the city and head to Snagov Monastery, a serene island retreat on Lake Snagov. Explore the medieval monastery, admire the beautiful frescoes, and enjoy the tranquility of the surroundings.
- **Alternative:** Embark on a scenic hike in Piatra Craiului National Park, just outside Bucharest. Breathe in the fresh mountain air, admire the

breathtaking views, and reconnect with nature's beauty.

Day 6: Embracing Local Traditions and Personal Rituals

- **Morning:** Visit the Village Museum, an open-air haven showcasing traditional Romanian houses, crafts, and folk art. Learn about local customs and traditions, and appreciate the simple beauty of life.
- **Afternoon:** Participate in a traditional pottery workshop and create your own souvenir to remember your trip.

Chapter 12

Getting Around

- Public Transportation Options

B
ucharest boasts a comprehensive public transportation network that can whisk you around the city efficiently and affordably. Here's a breakdown of your options:

- **Metro:** Bucharest's Metro is the fastest and most convenient way to navigate the city. Four lines (M1, M2, M3, M4) cover a large portion of the city, with extensions and new lines continuously under construction. Tickets are inexpensive and can be purchased at vending machines in stations.
- **Buses:** Bucharest has an extensive bus network with hundreds of lines reaching every corner of the city. Buses are generally slower than the Metro but offer wider coverage and run frequently. Validate your ticket upon boarding at the designated machines.
- **Trams and Trolleybuses:** Trams and trolleybuses offer another layer to the network, serving specific districts and providing a charming way to

experience the city. Fares and ticketing are the same as on buses.

- **Night Buses:** For late-night adventures, Bucharest operates a network of night buses (N1 - N122) connecting major points across the city. Night buses run hourly from Piata Unirii, making them convenient for post-nightlife adventures.
- **Single Tickets and Travel Cards:** Single tickets are valid for one journey on any mode of transport and can be purchased at vending machines or from drivers on buses and trams. For frequent travelers, consider day passes (valid for 24 hours) or multi-day passes (valid for 72 hours) offering unlimited travel on all public transport.

Tips for using Bucharest's Public Transport:

- Download the "STB București" app for real-time schedules, route planning, and ticket purchases.
- Validate your ticket upon boarding buses, trams, and trolleybuses.
- Metro stations and some buses may be crowded during peak hours.
- Be aware of pickpockets, especially in crowded areas.
- Don't hesitate to ask locals or station staff for assistance if you're unsure of directions.

Additional options:

- Taxis and Ridesharing: While public transport is generally efficient, taxis and ridesharing apps like Uber and Bolt can be helpful for late-night travel or reaching specific destinations.
- Bicycles: Bucharest offers a growing network of bike paths, and several bike rental companies operate within the city. Cycling can be a pleasant way to explore the city, though be mindful of traffic conditions.

With its diverse and affordable public transportation options, Bucharest makes getting around a breeze. So, hop on a bus, tram, or Metro train and embark on your exploration of this vibrant city!

- Renting a Car

Renting a car in Bucharest can be a convenient way to explore the city and surrounding areas at your own pace. However, there are some things you need to know before hitting the road. Here's a comprehensive guide to help you navigate the process:

Rules and Regulations:

- **Minimum age:** The minimum age to rent a car in Romania is 18, though some companies might require drivers to be 21 or 25 for specific car categories.
- **International Driving Permit:** If your driver's license is not in Romanian or Latin script, you'll need an International Driving Permit (IDP) alongside your valid license.
- **Speed limits:** Speed limits vary depending on the type of road. Generally, it's 50 km/h in urban areas, 90 km/h on national roads, and 130 km/h on motorways.
- **Parking:** Pay attention to parking signs and markings. On-street parking is often metered or requires permits. Use designated parking lots to avoid fines.
- **Drinking and driving:** The legal alcohol limit in Romania is 0.0%, so avoid driving after consuming any alcohol.
- **Mandatory equipment:** Seatbelts are mandatory for all passengers. Headlights must be used during low-visibility conditions and at night. Winter tires are required from November 1st to March 31st.

Fees:

- **Rental fees:** Prices vary depending on the car type, rental duration, and company. Compare quotes from different companies to find the best deal.
- **Insurance:** Rental car insurance is usually included in the base price, but consider additional coverage for peace of mind.

- **Fuel:** Prices are comparable to other European countries. Fuel stations are readily available throughout the city.
- **Tolls:** There are tolls on some motorways and bridges. Ensure you have the necessary toll stickers or cash beforehand.
- **Parking fees:** Parking rates vary depending on the location and duration. Look for parking meters or pay at designated booths.

How to Rent a Car:

- **Booking in advance:** Especially during peak season, consider booking your car online in advance to secure availability and potentially benefit from better deals.
- **Comparison websites:** Utilize comparison websites like Kayak, Rental-cars.com, or Skyscanner to compare prices and rental conditions from different providers.
- **Local rental companies:** Consider local companies alongside international brands, as they might offer more competitive rates and better local knowledge.
- **Read the fine print:** Carefully review the rental agreement before signing, paying attention to insurance coverage, fuel policy, and any additional fees.

Necessary Details:

- Valid driver's license and IDP (if applicable)
- Credit card (debit cards might not be accepted)
- Passport or another form of identification
- Proof of address (e.g., utility bill)
- Travel insurance (optional, but recommended)

Additional Tips:

- Familiarize yourself with the Romanian road signs and traffic regulations.

- Download offline maps or a GPS app to avoid navigation issues.
- Keep emergency contact information readily available.
- Check the weather conditions before your trip, as some mountain roads might be closed in winter.
- Enjoy the scenic drives and explore charming countryside villages and towns off the beaten path.

By following these tips and staying informed about the rules and regulations, renting a car in Bucharest can be a smooth and enjoyable experience. Take the wheel and discover the vibrant city and captivating landscapes of Romania at your own pace!

13

Chapter 13

Local Events and Festivals

- Annual Calendar of Events

Bucharest, Romania's pulsating capital, is a cultural kaleidoscope brimming with vibrant events throughout the year. From traditional celebrations to contemporary gatherings, there's something for every taste and interest. So, mark your calendars and prepare to immerse yourself in the city's infectious energy!

January:

- **New Year's Eve Celebrations:** Ring in the New Year with dazzling fireworks over Piața Constituției, live music performances, and festive cheer throughout the city.

February:

- **Valentine's Day:** Indulge in romantic dinners, special offers at spas and restaurants, and heartfelt performances.

- **International Fashion Week:** Witness the crème de la crème of Romanian and international fashion designers showcase their latest collections.

March:

- **Mărțișor Festival:** Welcome spring with the traditional exchange of "Mărțișoare," red and white talismans symbolizing good luck and health.
- **International Theatre Festival UNITER:** Experience a diverse range of theatrical performances from across the globe.

April:

- **Easter Celebrations:** Participate in traditional church services, savor festive dishes, and witness the vibrant egg-painting traditions.
- **Bucharest International Marathon:** Lace up your running shoes and test your endurance in this scenic race through the city streets.

May:

- **International Museum Night:** Explore Bucharest's museums after dark with extended hours, special exhibits, and engaging activities.
- **George Enescu Festival:** Immerse yourself in the world of classical music with concerts by renowned musicians and orchestras.

June:

- **SAGA Music Festival:** Groove to the beats of international and local DJs at this electrifying electronic music festival.
- **Bucharest Open Air Film Festival:** Enjoy a unique cinematic experience under the stars with screenings in parks and public squares.

July:

- **International Jazz Festival:** Delight in the smooth sounds of jazz legends and rising stars at this renowned festival.
- **Summer in the Parks:** Picnic, attend open-air concerts, and participate in fun activities during this series of vibrant events in Bucharest's green spaces.

August:

- **Beer Festival:** Raise a toast to craft beers from Romania and around the world at this lively festival with live music and delicious food.
- **Assumption of the Virgin Mary:** Witness religious processions and participate in traditional festivities around churches and monasteries.

September:

- **Festival of Wine and Cheese:** Sample gourmet wines and cheeses from Romanian producers at this delectable event.
- **Bucharest Fashion & Design Week:** Immerse yourself in the world of fashion and design with runway shows, exhibitions, and workshops.

October:

- **International Festival of Contemporary Dance:** Witness innovative and boundary-pushing dance performances from local and international companies.
- **Halloween Celebrations:** Get into the spooky spirit with costume parties, themed events, and haunted house experiences.

November:

- **Bucharest International Film Festival:** Discover acclaimed independent films and attend Q&A sessions with filmmakers and actors.
- **Black Friday Sales:** Take advantage of incredible deals on everything from

electronics to clothing at Bucharest's shops and malls.

December:

- **Christmas Markets:** Immerse yourself in the festive magic of Bucharest's Christmas markets, adorned with twinkling lights, traditional crafts, and delicious treats.
- **New Year's Eve Celebrations:** Raise a toast to the year gone by and welcome the new with dazzling fireworks, parties, and joyous anticipation.

14

Chapter 14

Sustainability and Responsible Tourism

- Eco-Friendly Practices and Supporting Local Communities

Bucharest is embracing a growing eco-conscious movement, offering plenty of ways for visitors to be responsible tourists and support local communities. Here are some ideas to incorporate eco-friendly practices and support local businesses during your stay:

Eco-Friendly Practices:

- **Stay Green:** Choose a hotel or guesthouse with sustainability practices like energy efficiency, water conservation, and waste reduction. Consider eco-friendly guesthouses like Green Hostel or Casa Mica Boutique Hotel.
- **Public Transportation:** Ditch the taxi and explore the city on foot, bike, or use the extensive public transportation network. Purchase a travel card for unlimited rides and reduce your carbon footprint.
- **Shop Local:** Skip the chain stores and head to farmers' markets like Piața Obor or Floreasca to support local farmers and vendors. Stock up on fresh produce, artisan crafts, and unique souvenirs.

- **Eat Consciously:** Opt for restaurants using local, seasonal ingredients and supporting sustainable farming practices. Try "Hanu' lui Manuc" for traditional Romanian cuisine with a modern twist.
- **Reduce Waste:** Bring your own reusable water bottle and shopping bag to minimize plastic waste. Choose restaurants with reusable dishes or biodegradable packaging.
- **Explore Green Spaces:** Escape the city bustle and recharge in Bucharest's many parks and gardens. Herastrau Park or Carol Park offer perfect spots for picnics, bike rides, or simply breathing in fresh air.
- **Responsible Hiking:** If venturing outside the city, stick to designated trails and minimize disturbance to wildlife and ecosystems. Leave no trace and pack out all your trash.

Supporting Local Communities:

- **Stay in Local Neighborhoods:** Avoid the tourist traps and choose accommodation in vibrant local districts like Victoriei or Dorobanți. This supports local businesses and allows you to experience authentic Romanian life.
- **Eat and Shop Locally:** Patronize independent restaurants and cafes run by local families. Browse local art galleries and craft shops for unique souvenirs.
- **Take Local Tours:** Choose tours led by local guides who can share insightful stories and insider tips about the city. Explore with "Bucharest Beyond the Walls" or "Taste of Bucharest" tours.
- **Learn Romanian Phrases:** Make an effort to learn basic Romanian greetings and phrases. Locals appreciate the gesture and you'll have a more authentic experience.
- **Volunteer:** Contribute to your community by volunteering at an organization like "Societatea Națională Crucea Roșie din România" or "The Hope and Homes for Children Foundation."
- **Donate to Local Causes:** Donate to local charities or support community projects that resonate with you.

By making these conscious choices, you can significantly reduce your environmental impact, contribute to the local economy, and create a more rewarding travel experience in Bucharest. Remember, small changes can make a big difference!

15

Conclusion

- Fond Farewell to Bucharest

Bucharest, with its vibrant tapestry woven from history, culture, and captivating energy, has embraced you, enchanted you, and left its mark upon your soul. As you stand at the crossroads of departure, a bittersweet symphony plays within.

Here's a melody to capture the essence of your fond farewell:

The city whispers goodbyes,Not in sorrow, but in sighs.Cobblestone streets etch memories,Of laughter, wonder, and mysteries.

From palaces that whisper tales,To hidden alleys, fortune sails.Each sunset painted the sky gold,As stories in your heart unfold.

You walked in Herastrau's verdant arms,Heard echoes of forgotten psalms.Savored sarmale's rich embrace,Danced the night in Bucharest's grace.

But now the plane's wing beckons near,A whisper soft, a time to hold

dear.Though miles may stretch, the ties remain,For Bucharest has etched your name.

So take a breath, one final glance,At gilded domes and Danube's chance.Promise not to fade, to come again,Where Bucharest, your friend, will grin.

Farewell, then, city of delight,May stars above guide you through night.Carry Bucharest within your heart,Till paths converge, a wondrous start.

Remember, Bucharest is not just a city, it's an experience. Carry the warmth of its people, the echoes of its laughter, and the vibrancy of its spirit wherever you go. It will wait for you, patiently nestled in the bend of the Danube, ready to welcome you back with open arms, another chapter waiting to be written in your shared story.

May your farewell be bittersweet, your memories vibrant, and your return inevitable.

Afterword

To make our learning experience enjoyable and safe, let's focus on practical and fun phrases that will help you navigate your travels in Romania. Here are a few ideas to get you started:

Greetings and Essentials:

- **Bună ziua!** (Good day!)
- **Mulțumesc!** (Thank you!)
- **Te rog!** (Please!)
- **Nu înțeleg.** (I don't understand.)
- **Vorbiți engleză?** (Do you speak English?)

Useful Phrases:

- **Cât costă?** (How much does it cost?)
- **Vreau să...** (I want to...)
- **Unde este...?** (Where is...?)
- **Pot să am...?** (May I have...?)
- **Puțină apă, vă rog.** (A little water, please.)

Fun Phrases:

- **Sunteți drăguț/drăguță!** (You're kind!)
- **Mâncarea este delicioasă!** (The food is delicious!)
- **Mi-a plăcut mult!** (I enjoyed it very much!)
- **La revedere!** (Goodbye!)

Remember, practice makes perfect, so don't be afraid to try out your new phrases with locals. They'll appreciate your effort and you'll be rewarded with genuine smiles and maybe even a new friend!

Have a wonderful and safe trip to Romania!